Garden
Almanac

2024

Quarto

First published in 2023 by Frances Lincoln,
an imprint of Quarto
1 Triptych Place,
London, SE1 9SH,
United Kingdom

www.Quarto.com

ISBN 978-0-7112-8900-0
Ebook ISBN 978-0-7112-8901-7

RHS Books Publishing Manager: Helen Griffin
RHS Head of Editorial: Tom Howard
RHS Books Editor: Simon Maughan
RHS Senior Wildlife Specialist: Helen Bostock
Authors: Zia Allaway and Guy Barter
Designer: Sarah Pyke

Printed in China

The Royal Horticultural Society is the UK's
leading gardening charity dedicated to
advancing horticulture and promoting good
gardening. Its charitable work includes
providing expert advice and information in
print, online and at its five major gardens and
annual shows, training gardeners of every age,
creating hands-on opportunities for children to
grow plants and sharing research into plants,
wildlife, wellbeing and environmental issues
affecting gardeners. For more information visit
www.rhs.org.uk or call 020 3176 5800.

MIX
Paper | Supporting
responsible forestry
FSC® C016973

Garden Almanac

2024

A seasonal guide to growing, harvesting and enjoying nature

Zia Allaway and Guy Barter

Introduction

Celebrating the gardening year, the *Garden Almanac 2024* offers a month-by-month guide to what to grow and how to maintain your plot, and much more besides. Written by Royal Horticultural Society and gardening experts, the book combines planting guides with entertaining facts about garden history and folklore.

Browse the pages to discover the average rainfall and hours of sun your local area experiences at different times of the year. This information will help you to plan your planting and irrigation needs as the seasons turn. Moon phases are also included, since moonlight can influence the activity of garden wildlife, such as some herbivorous insects which feed more heavily when the moon is bright. The easy, practical seasonal projects are designed to inspire you, while the recipes will help you make the most of your monthly harvests.

You can also learn about the different types of wildlife that may visit your garden throughout the year, and the roots of traditional festivals such as Halloween and Yule. There is space at the back of the book for your notes, too, where you can keep a record of what you have planted and sown, harvest times and your success rates.

Moon Phases

A Moon cycle, or a lunation, is the time it takes for the Moon to travel through its lunar phases and lasts about 29.5 days. Half of the Moon's surface is always illuminated by the sun, but the surface area we can see changes as it orbits the Earth. The eight phases in a lunar month are divided into four primary and four intermediate phases, as follows:

1 **NEW MOON** Primary phase, when the Moon is between the Sun and the Earth and cannot be seen because the whole surface is in shadow.

2 **WAXING CRESCENT MOON** Intermediate phase; the right half can be seen in the UK and in the Northern Hemisphere.

3 **FIRST QUARTER MOON (HALF MOON)** Primary phase: the right half of the Moon is illuminated in the UK and Northern Hemisphere.

4 **WAXING GIBBOUS MOON** Intermediate phase: the right half is illuminated in the UK and Northern Hemisphere.

5 **FULL MOON** Primary phase: the Moon and the Sun are on opposite sides of the Earth and the whole Moon is illuminated.

6 **WANING GIBBOUS MOON** Intermediate phase: the left half is lit in the UK and Northern Hemisphere.

7 **THIRD QUARTER MOON (HALF MOON)** Primary phase: the left half is lit in the UK and Northern Hemisphere.

8 **WANING CRESCENT MOON** Intermediate phase: the left half is lit in the UK and Northern Hemisphere.

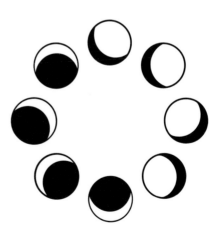

January

A month of new beginnings and remembering the year just past, January is named after the Roman god Janus whose two faces looked behind and ahead. While most of the garden slumbers under snow and ice, the perfume of sweet box and witch hazel flowers lingers on frost-laden air, reminding us that nature's gifts abound even in the depths of winter.

KEY EVENTS

New Year's Day, 1 January
Twelfth Night, 5 January
St Hilary's Day, 13 January *(said to be the coldest day of the year)*
Burns Night, 25 January

What to do

Although rain, snow and freezing temperatures often keep us indoors, there is still plenty to do in January. On milder days, planting bare-root or pot-grown trees and shrubs will help shake off the winter blues, while browsing nurseries' catalogues and websites on cold dark evenings heightens the anticipation for the months ahead. Cleaning sheds and greenhouses also makes good use of this quiet time in the garden.

In the garden

BARE-ROOT TREES, SHRUBS AND ROSES are available this month, and are generally cheaper than pot-grown plants. Plant them as soon as they arrive from the nursery unless the ground is frozen, in which case plant them temporarily in a sheltered area unaffected by ice, or in containers of potting compost in a greenhouse or shed until conditions improve (see p.216 on how to plant a tree). **❶**

CHECK TREE TIES and loosen any that are cutting into the stems. Also make sure that stakes are firmly secured and replace any that are broken.

ERECT A WINDBREAK around newly planted trees and shrubs to prevent damage to the roots or top growth. To create a temporary windbreak, hammer in sturdy posts on the side of the prevailing wind, and fix a semi-permeable trellis, split hazel panel, or similar screen to them that will filter 50 per cent of the wind. **❷**

PRUNE CLIMBERS, including wisteria, *Parthenocissus* species, climbing hydrangeas and ornamental vines (*Vitis coignetiae*). ❸

PLANT A HEDGE. You can order bare-root plants online and choose either a single species such as yew, or a mixture of different native trees and shrubs to create a wildlife hedge. Measure the length of the proposed hedge and calculate the quantity of plants you will need when they are spaced 45–60cm (18–24in) apart. To plant, dig a trench and set the plants at the same level as they were originally in the ground, indicated by the darker soil mark on the main stem.

BRUSH SNOW OFF conifers and evergreens, which may break under the weight, and from bird-proof netting in the vegetable garden.

TOP UP BIRD FEEDERS and provide fresh water frequently. Add a tennis ball to ponds, which will help to prevent them freezing over completely, or pour a little warm water around the edge to melt any ice that forms. ❹

In the fruit & veg patch

CHIT OR SPROUT EARLY SEED POTATOES by placing them in egg boxes or seed trays on a windowsill indoors with the eyes (bumps) facing upwards. They will soon sprout, ready to be planted outside in March.

PRUNE APPLE AND PEAR TREES Remove wayward and congested branches to create a balanced shape and open, airy framework. Call in a qualified arborist for large trees.

SOW MICROGREENS in shallow trays of moist compost in a bright spot indoors. They will germinate within days and offer fresh greens in about 6–8 weeks.

SOW EARLY CROPS INDOORS in modules or seed trays near a bright window in a warm room or in a heated greenhouse. Try spring onions, lettuces, summer cabbages, radishes, spinach, peas and broad beans, which will be ready to plant outside in spring.

PLANT GARLIC BULBS early in January in free-draining soil, setting them 15cm (6in) apart, with the tips 2.5cm (1in) below the soil surface.

USING A SLOW-RELEASE ORGANIC potassium-rich fertilizer, feed fruit trees and bushes at the end of the month.

Indoors

REDUCE WATERING, since most houseplants are dormant or semi-dormant in winter and need less moisture. Stop watering cacti and succulents altogether unless their leaves are starting to shrivel.

DO NOT FEED houseplants in winter.

BUY WINTER-FLOWERING indoor cyclamen and azaleas, Christmas cactus (*Schlumbergera*) and *Phalaenopsis* orchids to add colour to indoor displays.

TRANSFER FORCED NARCISSI and hyacinths that have finished blooming to a sheltered spot of the garden to die down – they may then reflower outside next year.

PROLONG POINSETTIA DISPLAYS by misting the leaves, watering only when the top of the compost feels dry, and keeping plants away from draughts.

Plant now

1. Fruit trees (such as apple trees)
2. Ornamental trees (such as *Pyrus elaeagrifolia* subsp. *kotschyana*)
3. Shrubs such as **mahonias**, dogwoods and viburnums.
4. Hedging plants (bare-root)
5. Roses (such as *Rosa* 'Coral Dawn')
6. Hellebores
7. Winter aconites (*Eranthis hyemalis*)
8. Early bulbous iris (in pots)
9. Sweet box (***Sarcococca hookeriana* var. *digyna*** and *S. confusa*)
10. Winter honeysuckle (*Lonicera × purpusii*)
11. Wintersweet (*Chimonanthus praecox*)

Project: Create a dead hedge

A dead hedge is easy to make, requires little ongoing maintenance and is the perfect way to create a decorative feature and wildlife habitat from garden waste. Composed of tree and shrub prunings knitted together to create a screen, it provides a great way to reuse material that would be difficult to compost if you don't own a shredder or would be a chore to take to the local recycling centre.

A dead hedge can also create a shelter belt for newly planted trees and shrubs, allowing wind to pass through it, and thus preventing turbulence that may damage your prized plants. It will also very slowly decompose, reducing in size naturally as your woody plants and trees grow while being sturdy enough to withstand blustery conditions.

Best suited to wildlife or informal gardens and small woodlands, a dead hedge is quick and easy to make. Simply hammer into the ground two parallel rows of upright wooden poles (available online), set out at 1.5m (5ft) intervals and to the required height. Then pile up tree and shrub prunings between the poles, placing the largest at the base and filling in spaces with smaller twigs and leaves. As the woody materials decompose, the hedge will reduce in height, but you can top it up annually with fresh prunings to maintain it. Prickly stems provide useful protection for nesting birds and hibernating amphibians such as toads. You can also allow ivy or a rambling rose to grow over your hedge to introduce a living element that will provide native animals with pollen-rich flowers and nutritious fruits.

Looking up

Sunrise and Sunset

While daylight hours are limited in January, the moon can often be seen for long periods during the night and day at this time of year.

	LONDON		EDINBURGH	
	Sunrise	Sunset	Sunrise	Sunset
Mon, Jan 1	8:03:59 am	4:03:41 pm	8:41:04 am	3:51:05 pm
Tue, Jan 2	8:03:53 am	4:04:44 pm	8:40:49 am	3:52:17 pm
Wed, Jan 3	8:03:43 am	4:05:49 pm	8:40:30 am	3:53:32 pm
Thu, Jan 4	8:03:30 am	4:06:57 pm	8:40:06 am	3:54:51 pm
Fri, Jan 5	8:03:14 am	4:08:07 pm	8:39:39 am	3:56:12 pm
Sat, Jan 6	8:02:55 am	4:09:20 pm	8:39:07 am	3:57:37 pm
Sun, Jan 7	8:02:32 am	4:10:35 pm	8:38:32 am	3:59:05 pm
Mon, Jan 8	8:02:06 am	4:11:53 pm	8:37:53 am	4:00:35 pm
Tue, Jan 9	8:01:37 am	4:13:12 pm	8:37:10 am	4:02:09 pm
Wed, Jan 10	8:01:05 am	4:14:34 pm	8:36:23 am	4:03:45 pm
Thu, Jan 11	8:00:29 am	4:15:58 pm	8:35:33 am	4:05:24 pm
Fri, Jan 12	7:59:51 am	4:17:23 pm	8:34:39 am	4:07:05 pm
Sat, Jan 13	7:59:09 am	4:18:51 pm	8:33:41 am	4:08:48 pm
Sun, Jan 14	7:58:25 am	4:20:20 pm	8:32:40 am	4:10:34 pm
Mon, Jan 15	7:57:37 am	4:21:51 pm	8:31:36 am	4:12:22 pm
Tue, Jan 16	7:56:46 am	4:23:23 pm	8:30:28 am	4:14:12 pm
Wed, Jan 17	7:55:53 am	4:24:57 pm	8:29:17 am	4:16:03 pm
Thu, Jan 18	7:54:57 am	4:26:33 pm	8:28:03 am	4:17:57 pm
Fri, Jan 19	7:53:58 am	4:28:10 pm	8:26:45 am	4:19:52 pm
Sat, Jan 20	7:52:56 am	4:29:48 pm	8:25:25 am	4:21:49 pm
Sun, Jan 21	7:51:52 am	4:31:27 pm	8:24:01 am	4:23:47 pm
Mon, Jan 22	7:50:45 am	4:33:07 pm	8:22:35 am	4:25:47 pm
Tue, Jan 23	7:49:35 am	4:34:49 pm	8:21:06 am	4:27:48 pm
Wed, Jan 24	7:48:23 am	4:36:31 pm	8:19:34 am	4:29:50 pm
Thu, Jan 25	7:47:09 am	4:38:14 pm	8:17:59 am	4:31:53 pm
Fri, Jan 26	7:45:52 am	4:39:58 pm	8:16:22 am	4:33:58 pm
Sat, Jan 27	7:44:33 am	4:41:43 pm	8:14:42 am	4:36:03 pm
Sun, Jan 28	7:43:11 am	4:43:29 pm	8:13:00 am	4:38:09 pm
Mon, Jan 29	7:41:47 am	4:45:15 pm	8:11:15 am	4:40:16 pm
Tue, Jan 30	7:40:21 am	4:47:01 pm	8:09:28 am	4:42:23 pm
Wed, Jan 31	7:38:53 am	4:48:48 pm	8:07:39 am	4:44:32 pm

Moonrise and moonset

Moon Phases

◑ **THIRD QUARTER** 4 January   ◐ **FIRST QUARTER** 18 January
● **NEW MOON** 11 January   ○ **FULL MOON** 25 January

MONTH	LONDON			EDINBURGH		
	Moonrise	Moonset	Moonrise	Moonrise	Moonset	Moonrise
1	-	11:06	21:52	-	11:28	21:58
2	-	11:17	23:02	-	11:33	23:13
3	-	11:26	05:22	-	11:38	
4	00:11	11:36		00:28	11:43	
5	01:23	11:48		01:45	11:49	
6	02:38	12:02		03:07	11:56	
7	03:57	12:20		04:33	12:08	
8	05:19	12:47		06:04	12:27	
9	06:40	13:27		07:32	13:00	
10	07:50	14:26		08:46	13:57	
11	08:44	15:45		09:35	15:21	
12	09:22	17:16		10:04	17:01	
13	09:48	18:50		10:21	18:44	
14	10:06	20:22		10:32	20:24	
15	10:21	21:50		10:40	21:59	
16	10:34	23:15		10:46	23:32	
17	10:47			10:53		
18		00:39	11:00		01:03	11:00
19	-	02:03	11:17	-	02:34	11:10
20	-	03:27	11:38	-	04:05	11:23
21	-	04:48	12:07	-	05:34	11:45
22	-	06:01	12:47	-	06:54	12:19
23	-	07:02	13:40	-	07:56	13:12
24	-	07:48	14:46	-	08:38	14:22
25	-	08:20	15:59		09:03	15:42
26	-	08:43	17:14	-	09:19	17:04
27	-	09:00	18:27	-	09:29	18:25
28	-	09:13	19:39	-	09:36	19:42
29	-	09:24	20:49	-	09:42	20:58
30	-	09:33	21:58	-	09:47	22:12
31	-	09:43	23:08	-	09:51	23:28

Average rainfall

In January, the average rainfall in the UK is 166mm (6.5in) but climate change has resulted in wide variations, with some years seeing dramatically more and others much less rain.

LOCATION	DAYS	MM	INCHES
Aberdeen	12	68	2.7
Aberystwyth	16	102	4
Belfast	14	88	3.5
Birmingham	13	72	2.8
Bournemouth	13	96	3.8
Bristol	13	82	3.2
Cambridge	10	48	1.8
Canterbury	12	64	2.5
Cardiff	16	127	5.0
Edinburgh	12	65	2.5
Exeter	13	97	3.8
Glasgow	17	147	5.8
Gloucester	13	78	3.0
Inverness	16	118	4.6
Ipswich	11	48	1.8
Leeds	16	109	4.3
Liverpool	13	69	2.7
London	12	70	2.75
Manchester	17	119	4.7
Newcastle upon Tyne	10	45	1.8
Norwich	11	55	2.2
Nottingham	12	59	2.3
Oxford	12	57	2.25
Sheffield	13	75	3.0
Truro	16	109	4.3

Feed the birds

Gardeners can help garden birds through the dead of winter by providing safe nesting sites and food, as well as planning and planting their outdoor spaces to deliver ample spring and summer supplies for fledglings.

Common garden birds resident in the UK include blackbirds, blue tits, coal tits, great tits, house sparrows, starlings and thrushes, which become more visible in January when the stems of deciduous shrubs and trees are bare and herbaceous plants have died back. In gardens near countryside, parks, canals or railways, bands of long-tailed tits and foraging parties of migratory fieldfares and redwings may also be seen now.

FOOD AND SHELTER

Winter is a good time to install nest boxes, and you can include a range of different styles and hole sizes to attract a diversity of birds. Hole sizes should be 25mm (1in) for blue tits and coal tits, 28mm (1.1in) for great tits, 32mm (1.3in) for house sparrows, and 45mm (1.8in) for starlings. Open-fronted boxes are favoured by robins and wagtails.

Unlike mammals, birds retain few fat reserves, and they spend most of their days searching for food. They also benefit from supplementary food which you can offer in special feeders or by scattering it on the ground or bird tables. Try berry cakes for finches; chopped cheese for wrens; fruit past its best to attract thrushes and blackbirds; nyger seeds for goldfinches; mealworms to lure robins; and peanuts for tits and starlings. Alternatively, use 'song bird' mixes. It is also important to offer clean water, especially in winter when natural sources may be frozen.

Unfortunately birds are sometimes prone to diseases (notably avian flu), so follow current advice from Defra to ensure disease is not inadvertently spread by garden bird feeding.

INSECT FEASTS

Birds synchronize their broods with insect abundance. While rich and varied plantings provide nectar and pollen for flying insects, they also support aphids, caterpillars and grubs that provide plentiful spring and summer food for birds and their young. Predatory insects, especially spiders, also make protein-rich bird food.

Encourage this insect bonanza with eryngiums and sunflowers, and berried shrubs such as berberis, cotoneaster, pyracantha and *Rosa rugosa*. Native trees, including crab apples, *Crataegus* (hawthorn), *Sorbus* (mountain ash and whitebeam) and eating apples are good choices, too, since they provide food for insect larvae that birds eat. Hedges also provide berries and cover, if cut lightly every two or three years, rather than annually. Hawthorn, hazel, holly and yew are good choices. Ivy is another great wildlife plant, the flowers supporting bees and the berries providing late winter food for birds, while teasels and devil's bit scabious are attractive seed-bearing wildflowers.

PERFECT TIMING

Did you know that birds have an inbuilt sense of time that drives their needs? Avian activity – from spring dawn choruses to nest building, egg laying and migration – is precisely timed over daily and annual scales. A complex interaction of the retina in the eyes, the hypothalamus (part of the brain), and especially the pineal gland measures day length, and this information modulates a bird's 'internal clock', so that birdsong begins at dawn each day. It also ensures that key activities such as breeding occur at the right time of year.

Edible garden

Despite the freezing temperatures and biting winds, a range of hardy vegetables stand strong and are ready to be harvested in January, while stored and preserved fruits offer a range of sweet treats.

Veg in season

CHARD, KALE AND WINTER CABBAGES provide nutritious leaves during the winter months.

BRUSSELS SPROUTS will still be delivering a crop this month. Remember to pick the sprouts from the bottom of the stem first.

LEEKS ARE IN SEASON, offering fresh, tangy stems to add to casseroles, stews and other warming winter dishes.

SPROUTING BROCCOLI is a great crop for small plots and can be harvested throughout the winter in mild regions if you plant hardy varieties.

ROOT CROPS including parsnips, turnips and celeriac are ready to harvest now. ❶

LETTUCES ARE SURPRISINGLY HARDY and if they are protected under a cloche or grown in a cold frame, you can pick fresh leaves throughout the winter months.

THE LAST OF THE RADISHES will also be available to add to salads.

POTATOES AND ONIONS that were harvested earlier and stored indoors (see p.202) also provide essential ingredients during this cold month.

HARVEST A FEW BAY AND ROSEMARY LEAVES from mature plants; make sure your herbs remain well covered with foliage, though, as they will not grow new leaves until spring.

Fruit in season

STORED FRUIT, such as apples and pears, offers a nutrient boost during January when few fresh fruits are in season. Check your stored produce regularly and remove any showing signs of mould or rot.

CONTINUE TO ENJOY RASPBERRIES that were harvested in the summer or autumn and frozen to retain their freshness (see p.134).

JAMS MADE EARLIER also bring the taste of summer to the winter table. ❷

FEELING ADVENTUROUS? Lemon trees (*Citrus × limon*) often come into fruit in late January. You will need a cool conservatory or heated greenhouse, where temperatures dip no lower than 10°C (50°F) at night, to grow a potted lemon tree over winter – heated rooms indoors will be too warm and dark, and plants are unlikely to fruit there. Water with tepid rainwater when the top of the compost feels dry, and mist plants every few days in the mornings throughout the year. Lemon trees can stand outside in summer. ❸

 # Recipe

POTATO AND LEEK GRATIN

This quick and simple recipe is the perfect way to use freshly harvested leeks and stored potatoes to warm up a cold winter's night. Serve the gratin as a main course or a side dish with fish or meat.

INGREDIENTS

2 leeks

3 tbsp unsalted butter, cut into chunks

1.5kg (3lb) potatoes

Salt and pepper to taste

180g (6oz) Gruyère or mature cheddar cheese, grated

Handful of chopped walnuts (optional)

1   Preheat the oven to 190°C (375°F/Gas 5). Clean the leeks and remove the root ends. Slice the white and dark green leaves and rinse in a colander to remove any grit or soil trapped between the layers.

2   Gently melt 2 tablespoons of the butter in a medium-sized frying pan. Add the leeks and fry for about 3 minutes, stirring frequently until they are wilted and soft. Set the leeks aside.

3   Rub the sides and base of a large baking tin with the remaining butter.

4   Peel the potatoes and, using a sharp knife or kitchen mandolin, cut them into 5mm (¼ in) slices. Cover the bottom of the baking tin with a quarter of the potato slices and sprinkle with salt and pepper. Spread half of the cooked leeks over the potatoes, then add another layer of potato slices, using the same quantity as before. Sprinkle half the cheese on top. Repeat these layers in the same order, so that you end with a topping of potatoes covered with cheese.

5   Cover the dish and bake for 20 minutes. Remove and uncover, then continue baking for about 25 minutes longer until the potatoes are soft when pierced with a fork and the cheesy topping is golden brown. Sprinkle the chopped walnuts on top if desired for added crunch.

Challenges of the month

Most pests will be inactive during January, but it's worth checking for snails and other overwintering pests in sheltered places, such as in or under empty pots in a cold frame, greenhouse or shed, or nestling behind benches and seats.

PREVENT ROOT AND STEM ROT developing on houseplants by reducing watering frequency in January when they are dormant or growing very slowly. Water only when the top of the compost feels bone dry and make sure your plants are in pots with drainage holes in the base. Also check that water does not collect in the outer waterproof container by removing the plant and watering it over the sink and leaving it to drain fully before replacing it. Cacti and most succulents will not require watering in winter, unless their leaves start to shrivel; if this occurs add a little moisture to remedy the problem.

CHECK HOUSEPLANTS FOR MEALYBUGS, which look like little beetles covered with a fluffy white wax, and hard bumps on stems that indicate scale insect infestation. Remove the pests with a damp cloth if possible, or, if only a few leaves and stems are affected, cut off the affected parts and place in your green waste collection bin.

PICK UP FALLEN LEAVES beneath roses and other disease-prone plants to reduce the spread of black spot, a soil-borne fungal infection. Bag up the leaves and take them to a local recycling centre or add to the green waste bin.

CLEAN ALL POTS AND SEED TRAYS with hot water and detergent to remove fungal spores and reduce the spread of bacterial diseases. After cleaning, try Citrox solution, a natural disinfectant containing citrus fruit extract.

ENTICE BIRDS INTO THE GARDEN to eat aphid eggs. These shiny black eggs will hatch into sap-sucking pests and may be found between the stems or bark crevices on fruit trees and roses. Try suspending fat balls from bamboo canes or wires to attract birds.

Look out for

The starling

A medium-sized, unassuming bird, an individual starling (*Sturnus vulgaris*) is easily overlooked, but take a closer look at an adult and you will see its black plumage is in fact a beautiful shimmering confection of purples and greens with pale spots. Flocks of starlings used to be a common site throughout the UK, but populations have plummeted in some areas in recent years and they are now on the Red List, which means they are of high conservation concern.

These feisty, gregarious birds are most abundant in southern England and you will probably see them in the garden during the winter, when huge roosts form at night in the countryside and city centres. January is also one of the best times to witness their spectacular aerial displays, known as murmurations, when just before sunset a thousand or more birds swirl and dance in unison, then fall like stones to the ground to roost in sheltered areas such as reedbeds and woodlands or close to buildings.

Flocking together offers the birds protection from predators such as peregrine falcons, while also providing additional warmth during the cold nights. Large numbers of starlings start to congregate in November, with more and more birds joining each group as the months pass so that by January some flocks may comprise 100,000 individuals. They roost during the day in more exposed sites such as treetops and nest in holes in trees and buildings in April.

Identifying hellebores

Loved for their exquisite winter blooms, evergreen foliage and shade tolerance, hellebores are available in a kaleidoscope of colours to suit any garden scheme. Among the first to flower is the white Christmas rose (*Helleborus niger*) which is in bloom by late December. Others soon follow, decorating the January garden with elegant, rounded blooms. Cut off old or tatty foliage as the flowers open – new leaves will soon emerge to replace it. Hellebores are poisonous if eaten and there is a small chance of skin irritation if handled without gloves.

STINKING HELLEBORE
(*HELLEBORUS FOETIDUS*)
Green nodding flowers are matched with spiny foliage that has an unpleasant odour when crushed, hence the name.
H x S: 80 x 45cm (32 x 18in)

CHRISTMAS ROSE
(*HELLEBORUS NIGER*)
The Christmas rose's elegant white flowers often appear in late December or early January.
H x S: 30 x 45cm (12 x 18in)

LENTEN ROSE
(*HELLEBORUS × HYBRIDUS*)
A vast choice of hybrids is available in almost every colour, except blue, and some may start flowering in late January or early February.
H x S: up to 50cm x 45cm (20 x 18in)

HELLEBORUS STERNII
This species is popular for its spiny foliage and purple-tinted, creamy green flowers, which may not open until February.
H x S: 35 x 30cm (14 x 12in)

CORSICAN HELLEBORE
(*HELLEBORUS ARGUTIFOLIUS*)
Grown for its architectural spiny foliage as well as the pale green blooms, the Corsican hellebore will thrive in sun or part-shade.
H x S: 50 x 90cm (20 x 36in)

Garden tales

History: Sentry palm (*Howea forsteriana*)

The elegant Sentry or Kentia palm has long been a favourite houseplant in British homes, bringing a tropical note to brighten up the darkest of winter days. It is named after Lord Howe Island, a small volcanic island between Australia and New Zealand where it grows wild, while the epithet 'forsteriana' refers to the father and son naturalists Johann Reinhold and Georg Forster, who accompanied Captain Cook on his second voyage to the Pacific in 1772–1775. However, it was not until the 1870s, when plant hunters brought the seed to the UK and found that this palm, unlike many others, survived in the low light and cool temperatures here, that it became a must-have houseplant.

A royal seal of approval from Queen Victoria also fuelled a frenzy for Sentries – she used the palms to decorate her palaces and they were also placed around her coffin as she lay in state. Later, the plants adorned the fashionable Palm Courts at high-class hotels such as the Ritz in London and Plaza in New York. Little wonder, then, that these elegant palms were soon gracing the more modest establishments of anyone who could afford one. Today, their popularity endures; they are loved for their sculptural fronds and easy-going nature, which makes them the perfect low-maintenance houseplant for new and more experienced gardeners alike.

Legend: Wassailing

Wassailing is an ancient British tradition with its roots in pagan rituals, which is held on the 5th January, also known as Twelfth Night. The word 'wassail' is derived from the Old English 'wes hál', which means 'to be in good health' and wassailing or wasselling refers to people in the local community visiting orchards and singing to the trees and spirits to ensure a good harvest in the year to come. In return, the orchard owner offers them a drink of warm cider or perry from a communal wassail bowl or cup. The wassail King and Queen lead the song, and the Queen is then lifted into the tree to place toast soaked in wassail liquor among the branches as a gift to the good spirits.

The tradition developed in the centuries prior to the Industrial Revolution, when Christmas celebrations lasted for twelve days, with feasting and revels on the final day. Twelfth Night is the day before the Epiphany, which in the Christian church commemorates the Magi's visit to the baby Jesus and his baptism by John the Baptist. As well as a celebration, it was also viewed as an auspicious day when evil spirits were banished and thanks were given to

> The word 'wassail' is derived from the Old English 'wes hál', which means 'to be in good health'

the good spirits of the trees. While the tradition has largely died out, wassailing is still practised in some rural areas of Scotland and England, including the village of Wisley close to the famous RHS Garden in Surrey.

Another separate wassailing custom was for people to go door to door, singing and offering their neighbours an alcoholic drink from the wassail bowl in exchange for gifts – a tradition similar to carolling. In the Middle Ages, peasants in the wassail would visit the Lord of the Manor to receive food and drink in return for his blessing and good will.

February

Traditionally a time for romance, February heralds renewed fertility, as sap begins to rise, buds swell, and ponds play host to the amorous antics of mating frogs. Winter's chill is still with us, though, and only a few brave bulbs and plants dare push through the frozen ground, their colourful blooms sparkling like precious jewels in the unforgiving landscape.

KEY EVENTS

Candlemas Day, 2 February
Shrove Tuesday, 13 February
St Valentine's Day, 14 February
Masi Magham Hindu Festival, 24 February

What to do

With spring almost upon us and plants breaking into bud, February is a good time for early pruning and planting. Consider the wildlife in your garden, too, as birds begin their search for nesting sites and some solitary and honey bees venture out on mild, sunny days to sample pollen-rich blooms, which you can plant now in the ground or in pots to sustain them. It's also your last chance to order bare-root trees, shrubs and roses, which are best planted before the end of the month (see p.35).

In the garden

PLANT SNOWDROPS 'in the green' at the end of February, since these diminutive bulbs establish well when planted in leaf after their flowers have faded. Separate them into groups of three to five bulbs and plant so that the roots and white area of the stem are below the surface, then water in generously. ❶

PUT UP NEST BOXES in your garden. If you have space, try including boxes of different sizes to attract the widest range of birds and check the RSPB website (rspb.org.uk) for details of where and how to install them. Also put up bat boxes in trees or on house or garden walls; the Bat Conservation Trust (bats.org.uk) has details of how and where to install them.

CUT BACK DECIDUOUS GRASSES
Remove the old stems of *Miscanthus*, *Calamagrostis*, *Panicum*, *Hakonechloa* and *Molinia* that have been left to stand over winter, allowing new growth to push through.

SHAPE WINTER-FLOWERING DECIDUOUS SHRUBS such as witch hazel (*Hamamelis*), *Corylopsis* and winter honeysuckle (*Lonicera* × *purpusii*, ❷) when the blooms have faded. Remove dead, diseased and crossing stems, together with some older growth, to create an open structure.

CUT BACK DECIDUOUS SHRUBS that will flower later in the summer, such as *Buddleja*, *Leycesteria*, and *Hypericum*, removing old, dead and diseased growth and crossing stems. Leave those that will flower in the spring, as you may remove the flower buds.

START SOWING HALF-HARDY SUMMER ANNUALS, such as begonias, tobacco plants (*Nicotiana*), cosmos ❸ and lobelia, in late February in modules or seed trays on a warm windowsill or in a propagator in a heated greenhouse.

PRUNE LATE-FLOWERING CLEMATIS that bloom in or after July. Take all the stems down to 25cm (10in) from the ground and remove some of the old growth. After pruning, feed with a slow-release organic fertilizer and apply a mulch, ensuring it does not touch the stems. ❹

In the fruit & veg patch

SOW HARDY VEGETABLE SEEDS under cloches. Try lettuces, radishes, peas, broad beans, spring onions, beetroot, summer cabbages and spinach. Alternatively, start them off in pots in a coldframe or greenhouse.

PLANT GARLIC, SHALLOTS AND BROWN ONIONS in free-draining soil, setting them 15cm (6in) apart and in rows the same distance apart, with bulb tips just showing above the surface.

FEED SPRING CABBAGES with general purpose organic fertilizer. Harvest every other cabbage and leave the stubs in the ground, cutting a cross in the top. These will then develop into mini cabbages while the remaining plants grow into full-size crops.

PRUNE AUTUMN-FRUITING RASPBERRY CANES to the ground. Do not cut summer-fruiting raspberries until after they have cropped.

PLANT BARE-ROOT RASPBERRY AND BLACKBERRY BUSHES in weed-free soil as soon as they arrive. Attach wires to a wall or fence to support blackberry stems; raspberries prefer more air around them, so create a support using a pair of horizontal wires attached to two sturdy posts on either side of the row of canes.

Indoors

KEEP HOUSEPLANTS on the dry side throughout the winter; wait until the temperature and light levels increase next month.

DIVIDE *BEGONIA REX* and other tuberous evergreen begonias. Tip the plant from its pot and brush off the compost to expose the tuber. Remove the leaves, then cut the tuber into pieces, each with a few roots. Replant the pieces in pots on a bed of compost mixed with horticultural sand, covering them lightly. Keep moist but not wet.

PRUNE TENDER PERENNIALS AND SHRUBS that are over wintering indoors, such as fuchsias, salvias, and pelargoniums. Remove dead, diseased, and old stems and then apply an all-purpose organic fertilizer.

Plant now

1. Bare-root and pot-grown shrubs (such as *Camellia × williamsii* 'Anticipation')
2. *Clematis cirrhosa* var. purpurascens 'Lansdowne Gem'
3. *Cornus mas*
4. *Cyclamen coum*
5. *Daphne odora* variegata
6. *Galanthus* (snowdrop) (see p.47)
7. *Hacquetia epipactis*
8. *Leucothoe* Scarletta ('Zeblid')
9. *Mahonia × media*
10. *Stachyurus praecox*
11. Hardy perennials (such as *Pulmonaria*)

Project: Easy terrarium

These glass jars filled with leafy plants make a beautiful feature for any room that receives some sun, and they're very easy to make and maintain. Choose from a range of slow-growing tropical foliage plants for a terrarium with a closed lid, or succulents and cacti for an open-topped container. You can make your terrarium in any glass container with an opening that's large enough to get your hands in, such as a pasta jar, Kilner jar, fishbowl, aquarium or even a large jam jar.

Next, decide which types of plant you want to include. Do not mix tropicals with succulents – they like different soil types and humidity levels. Good tropical choices include *Fittonia, Pilea, Hypoestes phyllostachya,* and *Peperomia* and ferns such as *Adiantum raddianum, Pteris* and *Asplenium.* Any small succulents or cacti will work in an open terrarium.

Add a 5cm (2in) drainage layer of small pebbles or horticultural grit to the bottom of your container, followed by a 2cm (½in) layer of activated charcoal, which helps to prevent bacterial growth. Over this, add a layer of houseplant or cactus compost, depending on which plants you're using, that's deep enough to cover their roots. When planting, make sure you do not bury the stems and leaves, and firm the compost gently around the roots to remove large air gaps. Avoid overfilling the terrarium, leaving space for each plant to grow. Finally, add a layer of moss from the garden (for tropicals) or gravel around the plant stems. Using a water spray or small can fitted with a rose head, water the soil until damp but not wet. Add a lid to a tropical terrarium, which will keep the plants moist for many weeks, removing it about once a month to allow condensation to escape. If your plants start to rot, you have added too much water, so leave it until the compost is dry before watering again. For succulents and cacti, water very sparingly, and only water again when the soil layer feels completely dry. Set your terrarium in a bright spot out of direct sunlight; succulents will need more sun than most tropical plants.

Looking up

Sunrise and Sunset

The days become noticeably longer as the month progresses. Growth can be slow with low temperatures and low light, but warmth starts to accumulate in soil and plants.

	LONDON		EDINBURGH	
	Sunrise	Sunset	Sunrise	Sunset
Thu, Feb 1	7:37:23 am	4:50:36 pm	8:05:48 am	4:46:40 pm
Fri, Feb 2	7:35:51 am	4:52:24 pm	8:03:54 am	4:48:50 pm
Sat, Feb 3	7:34:17 am	4:54:12 pm	8:01:59 am	4:50:59 pm
Sun, Feb 4	7:32:40 am	4:56:01 pm	8:00:01 am	4:53:09 pm
Mon, Feb 5	7:31:03 am	4:57:50 pm	7:58:02 am	4:55:20 pm
Tue, Feb 6	7:29:23 am	4:59:39 pm	7:56:01 am	4:57:30 pm
Wed, Feb 7	7:27:41 am	5:01:28 pm	7:53:58 am	4:59:41 pm
Thu, Feb 8	7:25:58 am	5:03:17 pm	7:51:53 am	5:01:52 pm
Fri, Feb 9	7:24:13 am	5:05:07 pm	7:49:46 am	5:04:03 pm
Sat, Feb 10	7:22:27 am	5:06:56 pm	7:47:38 am	5:06:14 pm
Sun, Feb 11	7:20:39 am	5:08:45 pm	7:45:28 am	5:08:25 pm
Mon, Feb 12	7:18:49 am	5:10:35 pm	7:43:17 am	5:10:36 pm
Tue, Feb 13	7:16:58 am	5:12:24 pm	7:41:04 am	5:12:47 pm
Wed, Feb 14	7:15:06 am	5:14:13 pm	7:38:50 am	5:14:58 pm
Thu, Feb 15	7:13:12 am	5:16:02 pm	7:36:35 am	5:17:09 pm
Fri, Feb 16	7:11:17 am	5:17:51 pm	7:34:18 am	5:19:19 pm
Sat, Feb 17	7:09:20 am	5:19:40 pm	7:32:00 am	5:21:30 pm
Sun, Feb 18	7:07:23 am	5:21:29 pm	7:29:41 am	5:23:40 pm
Mon, Feb 19	7:05:24 am	5:23:17 pm	7:27:20 am	5:25:50 pm
Tue, Feb 20	7:03:24 am	5:25:06 pm	7:24:59 am	5:28:00 pm
Wed, Feb 21	7:01:23 am	5:26:54 pm	7:22:36 am	5:30:10 pm
Thu, Feb 22	6:59:21 am	5:28:42 pm	7:20:13 am	5:32:19 pm
Fri, Feb 23	6:57:18 am	5:30:29 pm	7:17:48 am	5:34:28 pm
Sat, Feb 24	6:55:14 am	5:32:17 pm	7:15:22 am	5:36:37 pm
Sun, Feb 25	6:53:09 am	5:34:04 pm	7:12:56 am	5:38:46 pm
Mon, Feb 26	6:51:03 am	5:35:51 pm	7:10:28 am	5:40:54 pm
Tue, Feb 27	6:48:56 am	5:37:37 pm	7:08:00 am	5:43:02 pm
Wed, Feb 28	6:46:48 am	5:39:23 pm	7:05:31 am	5:45:10 pm
Thu, Feb 29	6:44:40 am	5:41:09 pm	7:03:01 am	5:47:17 pm

Moonrise and moonset

Moon Phases

◑ **THIRD QUARTER** 2 February   ◐ **FIRST QUARTER** 16 February
● **NEW MOON** 9 February   ○ **FULL MOON** 24 February

FEB	LONDON			EDINBURGH		
	Moonrise	Moonset	Moonrise	Moonrise	Moonset	Moonrise
1	-	09:53			09:56	
2	00:20	10:06		00:47	10:03	
3	01:36	10:21		02:09	10:12	
4	02:55	10:43		03:36	10:26	
5	04:15	11:15		05:04	10:51	
6	05:29	12:04		06:25	11:33	
7	06:31	13:12		07:25	12:44	
8	07:16	14:38		08:03	14:18	
9	07:47	16:13		08:24	16:03	
10	08:09	17:49		08:38	17:47	
11	08:25	19:22		08:47	19:28	
12	08:39	20:52		08:54	21:06	
13	08:52	22:20		09:01	22:41	
14	09:06	23:47		09:08		
15	09:21				00:16	09:17
16		01:14	09:41		01:50	09:29
17		02:38	10:07		03:22	09:47
18		03:54	10:44		04:46	10:17
19		04:59	11:34		05:54	11:04
20		05:49	12:36		06:41	12:09
21		06:24	13:47		07:10	13:27
22		06:49	15:01		07:28	14:49
23		07:07	16:15		07:39	16:10
24		07:21	17:27		07:46	17:29
25		07:32	18:38		07:52	18:45
26		07:42	19:47		07:57	20:00
27		07:51	20:57		08:01	21:15
28		08:01	22:08		08:06	22:32
29		08:12	23:22		08:11	23:53

Average rainfall

The February average rainfall for the UK is 120mm (4.7in), but there are dramatic differences throughout the country, with regions of high ground in the west receiving almost double that of locations in the east. Soil is usually saturated by now, so gardening is on hold until it dries out.

LOCATION	DAYS	MM	INCHES
Aberdeen	11	59	2.3
Aberystwyth	14	98	3.8
Belfast	13	70	2.75
Birmingham	10	55	2.2
Bournemouth	11	67	2.6
Bristol	10	58	2.3
Cambridge	9	36	1.4
Canterbury	9	50	2.0
Cardiff	12	93	3.7
Edinburgh	10	53	2.1
Exeter	14	133	5.2
Glasgow	15	115	4.5
Gloucester	11	66	2.6
Inverness	12	61	2.4
Ipswich	9	42	1.6
Leeds	13	89	3.5
Liverpool	12	57	2.2
London	11	51	2.0
Manchester	14	97	3.8
Newcastle upon Tyne	9	41	1.6
Norwich	11	45	1.8
Nottingham	11	50	2.0
Oxford	9	47	1.8
Sheffield	11	67	2.6
Truro	13	83	3.3

Buying and making composts

The potting compost buying season approaches as gardeners plan to sow seeds, pot up plants and cuttings, and refill containers, and there are a few reasons why this growing medium is used, rather than garden soil.

Soils are a mix of minerals, organic matter, water and air. Despite holding their structure in the open ground due to natural processes, they often fall short when used in pots and containers. This is because the soil can become compacted and the air spaces squeezed out. The air content is essential for plant growth and the most important element in a potting compost. Garden soil is also potentially contaminated with weed seeds and disease organisms.

HEALTHY AIR

To overcome this problem, gardeners have traditionally made or bought 'potting composts' that contain more organic matter than is usually found in garden soil. In fact, these products are not actually compost at all, but a mix of materials formulated for the right friable and free-draining consistency. The organic matter provides the air spaces and, therefore, the drainage also required in pots, allowing oxygen to enter and promoting healthy root growth. Organic matter also retains plant nutrients just like fertile soil.

ADDED EXTRAS

Composts contain a range of non-soil components, too, traditionally including peat – which is strictly avoided nowadays as peat extraction is damaging to the environment – sand, grit, composted municipal green waste, wood fibre, coir (coconut fibre) and bark. Fertilizer and lime are also added to achieve the optimum nutrient levels and acidity (pH value). Commercial potting composts sold in garden centres are often formulated for particular purposes, such as for houseplants, seed sowing, cuttings or vegetables, but many are branded 'multipurpose' and designed to be good enough for most uses. Check the labels carefully, however, as some may not be suitable for seeds, and choose a product appropriate to your needs. It is also a good idea to look for packaging dates on the sides of bags. Potting compost contains lots of organic matter, which degrades over time, so fresher is better.

REUSING OLD POTTING COMPOST

Any surplus potting compost left over from the previous year can be mixed in equal parts with new material and will be good enough for less demanding plants. Adding small, chipped bark to old potting compost can inject air spaces and is worth considering for larger containers. Alternatively, use old potting compost as a mulch or soil improver.

MAKING YOUR OWN

While it's fun to make your own potting composts, it can also be potentially risky, particularly for seed sowing since germination is dependent on the right growing conditions. Despite this, some gardeners claim good results with mixes of homemade garden compost, leaf mould, sieved garden soil, sand and grit.

The risks are lower if you need compost for larger containers filled with young or more mature plants. Here, you can make significant savings by making your own, and it should not affect the health of your plants. A mixture of two parts garden soil and one part homemade compost is worth experimenting with, perhaps adding some sand if your garden soil is rich in clay.

Edible garden

Cold, wintry weather is still with us in February, but many hardy crops stand strong, ready to be harvested as winter ends.

Veg in season

CHARD, KALE, WINTER CABBAGES and Brussels sprouts continue to provide fresh vitamin-rich greens to steam or add to soups and casseroles. **❶**

CAULIFLOWERS will provide a crop this month in mild regions. You can also sow summer varieties indoors in modules; wait until May to sow autumn crops.

SPROUTING BROCCOLI and leeks are still in season in February.

CELERIAC IS A DELICIOUS ROOT CROP that delivers throughout winter. An early spring sowing, with young crops planted out in June, will provide celery-flavoured roots from autumn. Leave plants in the ground and harvest as and when you need them.

STORED WINTER SQUASH AND ONIONS should still be good to eat. Keep squash in a cool, well-ventilated area above 10°C (50°F); onions will be fine stored in a shed.

FENNEL, PUMPKIN AND NIGELLA SEEDS that were dried and stored last summer and autumn add flavour and a nutrient boost to salads and stir fries in winter.

Fruit in season

LEMONS AND ORANGES, grown in a cool conservatory or a heated greenhouse over winter, will start to produce ripe fruit that's been developing for a few months. Do not expect a bumper crop, but a few home-grown juicy citrus fruits at this time of year are a real novelty.

STORED APPLES can be used to create sweet and savoury dishes this month. Check them regularly and compost any that show signs of decay. **❷**

FEELING ADVENTUROUS? The Chilean guava berry bush (*Ugni molinae*) produces bowl-shaped white or pink flowers in late spring followed by dark red sweet fruits that taste a little like strawberries. Hardy to about –10°C (14°F), it grows to a metre (3ft) in height and spread and needs acidic soil and a sunny, sheltered position to thrive. Plant it in a pot of ericaceous compost if you don't have the right soil or you live in an area that experiences cold winters, where it will need some winter protection.

 # Recipe

CRISPY KALE WITH SPICY FISHCAKES

This simple recipe makes good use of fresh kale leaves that can be harvested in February, while the fishcakes can be rustled up from store-cupboard ingredients in about 40 minutes.

1 Boil the potato in salted water for about 15 minutes until soft. Drain and allow to steam dry for a couple of minutes, then put in a bowl and mash with a potato masher or fork.

2 Mix the tuna, egg, onion, Dijon mustard, breadcrumbs, garlic, chilli, salt, and pepper into the mashed potato until all the ingredients are blended. Divide the mixture into 8 equal portions and shape into small patties.

3 Meanwhile, preheat the oven to 180°C (350°F/Gas 6). Spread the kale on a baking sheet and drizzle with olive oil. Mix the sugar and sesame seeds and sprinkle over the kale. Toss so all the leaves are covered and bake for about 5 minutes until crisp. Turn off the oven but leave the kale to keep warm.

4 Heat the remaining oil in a frying pan, and fry the fishcakes for about 3 minutes on a medium heat until brown and crisp.

5 Serve the kale and fishcakes on warmed plates.

INGREDIENTS

1 large floury potato, such as Maris Piper or King Edwards, peeled and cubed

3 x 140g (5oz) cans tuna in water, drained (check the package to ensure it has been sustainably sourced)

1 egg

I small onion, chopped

1 tbsp Dijon mustard

1 tbsp dry breadcrumbs, or as needed

1 garlic clove, finely chopped

½ dried chilli, finely chopped

Salt and ground black pepper to taste

Fresh kale leaves, washed and dried

2-3 tbsp olive oil

I tbsp soft brown sugar

I tbsp sesame seeds (optional)

Challenges of the month

While many small invertebrates will still be inactive in February, check for snails and other overwintering insects in sheltered places around the garden.

MICE, SQUIRRELS AND RATS are active all year round, looking for food and warm places to sit out the worst of the weather, so make sure your stored fruit and vegetables are in a secure place, out of their reach.

ENCOURAGE PREDATORS such as frogs and toads into your garden by making a small pond with sloping sides that offer them easy access to the water. These useful amphibians enjoy a meal of slugs and snails, and frogs will be lured to your pond this month to mate. Surround it with evergreen foliage plants that provide some cover for them as they hop out of the water. A pond will encourage birds, too.

REMOVE FUNGAL SPORES AND BACTERIAL INFECTIONS, as well as overwintering invertebrates, from seed trays and pots before the sowing season gets fully underway. Use hot soapy water to clean them and then apply a natural disinfectant such as Citrox solution. Leave them to dry in a warm area; do not stack while still damp.

CONTINUE TO CHECK HOUSEPLANTS for creatures such as mealybugs and scale insects (see p.245) and remove them as soon as possible before their numbers build up.

CHECK HOUSEPLANTS FOR PALE YELLOW LEAF SPOTS, which may be caused by cold conditions, if the room temperature falls too low overnight, or watering with cold water. Move the plant to a warmer spot away from draughts and leave tap water in the can for a few hours to take off the chill before watering. Remember, too, that most houseplants need very little moisture in winter while they are dormant or growing very slowly, and overwatering can lead to root and stem rot.

Look out for

The frog

Just as Valentine's Day celebrations get underway, frogs are also feeling amorous as their breeding season begins. You are most likely to spot the UK native common frog (*Rana temporaria*) in your garden, although the larger non-native marsh frog (*Pelophylax ridibundus*) is sometimes seen in the south-east of the country. The very rare pool frog (*Pelophylax lessonae*), thought to be extinct in the UK as recently as 1995, has been reintroduced to a site in East Anglia.

Common frogs have smooth skin, and are green to brown or even red or yellow in colour, with dark bands on their back legs. Pool frogs are brown or green, with dark spots on their backs, and two ridges running from each eye and a cream stripe down their backs. Marsh frogs are about 15cm (6in) or more in length and have warty green skin with irregular dark blotches.

These amphibians breed in ponds from February to March, where some will have spent the winter, surviving under the water by absorbing oxygen through their skin. You will notice a huge commotion in the water during February as the males wrap themselves around the females, using the 'nuptial pads' on their front feet to help them grip on. The females then lay large numbers of eggs (spawn) in jelly-like clumps just below the surface, after which common frogs retreat to dry land, where they spend most of the year hunting among the plants for slugs, snails, worms, flies and moths (marsh frogs stay in or close to the water throughout the year). About three weeks later, tadpoles will hatch, and they then take about 14 weeks to metamorphose into frogs.

Identifying snowdrops

The unfurling of this quintessential winter flower marks the turning of the seasons, as stems of tiny nodding white bells push up through frozen ground to herald the start of a new growing year. There are about 20 species of snowdrop native to Europe and the Middle East, the most common of which are *Galanthus nivalis, Galanthus elwesii* and *Galanthus plicatus,* and almost all the hybrids have been bred from these three. Snowdrops prefer a position in part shade and soil that doesn't bake in summer. Those listed here have all attained the RHS Award of Garden Merit. Snowdrops are poisonous if eaten.

COMMON SNOWDROP
(*GALANTHUS NIVALIS*)
One of the first snowdrops to flower, this classic beauty has simple white honey-scented blooms with small green markings on the inner segments.
H x S: 10 x 10cm (4 x 4in)

GIANT SNOWDROP
(*GALANTHUS WORONOWII*)
While the plant itself is not large, the clear white blooms are bigger than some other species and the leaves shiny and broader, hence the common name.
H x S: 15 x 5cm (6 x 2in)

PLEATED SNOWDROP
(*GALANTHUS PLICATUS*)
Named for its grey-green pleated leaves, this beautiful snowdrop produces single white flowers with green markings on the inner segments.
H x S: 20 x 5cm (8 x 2in)

GREATER SNOWDROP (*GALANTHUS ELWESII*)
Known for its glaucous leaves, which are folded one inside the other, and flowers with two large green spots and smaller markings on the inner segments.
H x S: 15 x 5cm (6 x 2in)

SNOWDROP 'S.ARNOTT'
(*GALANTHUS 'S.ARNOTT'*)
Taller and with larger flowers than the common snowdrop, this beautiful cultivar has similar single blooms with small green markings on the inner segments.
H x S: 25 x 10cm (10 x 4in)

Garden tales

History: The rise of the orangery

The sweet oranges we know and love today were first cultivated in Europe in the late 15th century or beginning of the 16th century, when Italian and Portuguese merchants brought the trees to the Mediterranean. Hailing from China, the juicy fruits thrived in the mild Southern European climate but they were unable to survive cold, wet British winters. Pioneering gardeners managed to cosset some under temporary covers, but it was not until the 17th century when glass-making technology allowed panels of clear glass to be produced that buildings with large, south-facing windows were constructed to house these tender beauties. Royals and aristocrats began building elaborate 'orangeries' for their prized fruit trees, which were a symbol of prestige and wealth; the plants were grown in tubs and overwintered inside and then set out in the garden during the summer months.

These beautiful glass-fronted buildings soon adorned the most fashionable country houses in Britain, including Ham House near Richmond, Hanbury Hall in Worcestershire, and Kew near Richmond, which boasted the largest orangery in England when it was built in 1761 by Sir William Chambers. However, orangeries' covered roofs meant that the light levels were never sufficient for plants to survive in them for long, so

when structures with glazed roofs were introduced in the early 19th century, offering better light conditions and higher temperatures, the orangery went out of fashion. Known as greenhouses or conservatories – 'green' describing the plants that were 'conserved' inside them – the new all-glass buildings allowed the cultivation of pineapples, grapes and a range of other tender fruits, as well as citrus. Despite no longer being used exclusively for plant cultivation, many orangeries were preserved as beautiful architectural rooms and a few still survive today.

Legend: Rose – the flower of love

The most anticipated day in February is the 14th, when lovers exchange cards and gifts, most notably red roses. The significance of the flowers, as well as Valentine's Day itself, are rooted in mythology and legend. The celebration is named after the Christian martyr Valentine, who was executed on the 14th February when he defied the Roman Emperor Claudius II by secretly performing marriage ceremonies for soldiers, which Claudius had banned because he thought they should love only Rome. Legend says that in 496 A.D. Pope Gelasius I announced that the 14th February would be St Valentine's Day, officially ending the older pagan Feast of Lupercalia, which was also held around this time to mark the beginning of spring. However, historians believe the origins of Valentine's Day may be much later than this.

The symbolism of the rose also dates back many centuries, while the colour red has long been associated with love and passion.

The symbolism of the rose also dates back many centuries, while the colour red has long been associated with love and passion. In Greek mythology, a white rose first appeared during the birth of Aphrodite, the goddess of sexual love and beauty, and while trying to save her lover, Adonis, who was mauled by a boar when out hunting, she cut her foot on the thorns as she rushed to warn him of the danger. Her blood spilled on to the white petals, staining them crimson, and so began the association between the red rose and passionate love.

In the 19th century, the Victorians believed that flowers and their colours held different meanings, many of which still stand today: red roses are symbolic of love and passion; yellow blooms signify friendship; orange roses symbolize desire; and pink flowers are given as thanks. The number twelve is also significant on this special day, being traditional to give a dozen roses to your loved one. It symbolizes the twelve months of the year and the number of zodiac signs.

March

The first month of spring is a time to celebrate, as the sun ascends higher in the sky and the garden brims with new life. Trees don veils of blossom while nodding daffodils usher in the season alongside pollen-rich primroses and pulmonarias, offering an early feast for the bees. There's still a bite in the air, though, as March winds buffet plants and birds alike.

KEY EVENTS
First day of meteorological spring, 1 March
First day of Ramadan, 11 March
St Patrick's Day, 17 March
Vernal equinox (*start of horticultural spring*) 20 March
Easter Day, 31 March

What to do

March is a busy time in the garden and indoors as seed-sowing begins in earnest. Early-spring weather is unpredictable, with mild sunny days followed by hard frosts and wintry showers, so while it's a good month for planting, only set out hardy plants that can tolerate low temperatures. Continue to prune late summer-flowering shrubs that bloom on the current season's growth (see p.33), sow half-hardy bedding (see p.33), and keep weeds at bay so they won't compete with your crops and flowers.

In the garden

DIVIDE LARGE CLUMPS OF PERENNIALS or container-grown plants that have outgrown their allotted space. Dig around the outside edge of the stems and lift them out. Use a sharp spade to cut through the clump or tease apart with a hand fork, or use a sharp knife or pruning saw to cut the clump into sections. Discard old stems (often in the middle of the clump) and replant the smaller groups where needed. **❶**

PLANT HARDY SHRUBS AND PERENNIALS, as well as hardy spring bedding such as wallflowers and forget-me-nots to plug the gaps with spots of colour.

CUT BACK ESTABLISHED SHRUBS GROWN FOR WINTER STEM INTEREST, such as *Cornus sanguinea, Cornus alba* and the willow *Salix alba,* in late March or early April. Take the stems back to about 30–45cm (12–18in) from the ground and use the prunings to make plant supports (see p.56). **❷**

ADD AN ORGANIC MULCH over the soil. Cover the surface with 5–7.5cm (2–3in) of soil conditioner or homemade compost, leaving a gap around shrubs and trees. This suppresses weeds and improves the soil structure, helping sandy types to retain more moisture and nutrients and heavy clays to drain more freely. ❸

PRUNE BUSH ROSES before the end of March, removing old, unproductive or diseased stems. For hybrid teas, cut the remaining stems down to four or six buds above the base of the previous year's growth (older brown wood). Prune the stems of floribundas to about 30cm (1ft) from the ground. ❹

SOW HARDY ANNUALS OUTSIDE where they are to grow. Remove weeds and large stones and rake the surface to form a bed of crumb-like soil. Avoid sowing close to trees and shrubs, which may cast too much shade for many annuals.

PLANT OUT SWEET PEAS that were sown in autumn and overwintered undercover – leave this job until next month if you live in a cold area.

KEEP WEEDS AT BAY by hoeing off annuals and digging out pernicious perennials, such as brambles, bindweed and ground elder. ❺

In the fruit & veg patch

SOW TOMATO SEEDS undercover in small pots or module trays. Keep moist and warm on a windowsill or in a heated greenhouse until they germinate.

FEED AND THEN ADD A MULCH of garden compost or soil conditioner around fruit bushes, such as raspberries, blackberries and currants.

PRICK OUT HARDY CROPS SOWN UNDERCOVER in February by transplanting the seedlings once they have a few sets of leaves into individual 9cm (3½in) biodegradable or recycled plastic pots. Leave to grow on inside, and plant out at the end of the month.

SOW BATCHES OF HARDY VEGETABLES such as lettuces, radishes, salad onions, peas, broad beans, spinach, cabbages and beetroot in situ outside in prepared beds. Once germinated and with a few leaves, thin to the final spacings given on individual seed packs.

Indoors

INCREASE WATERING OF HOUSEPLANTS this month, as they start showing signs of growth, but do not overdo it – make sure they are in pots with drainage holes in the base and are never left to sit in soggy compost.

BEGIN FEEDING HOUSEPLANTS in March using an all-purpose liquid organic fertilizer. Cacti and succulents will not need feeding just yet.

REMOVE DUST FROM THE LEAVES of plants with large shiny foliage using clean, tepid water. Never apply leaf shine or any other product that coats the surface, which may hamper photosynthesis, and don't wash plants with furry or hairy leaves – blow dust off or dislodge it gently with a soft cloth.

Plant now

1. Summer-flowering bulbs, such as **dahlias**, lilies and gladioli
2. Later-flowering hardy perennials and shrubs (such as *Helenium* 'Sundae')
3. Camellias
4. Sweet peas (*Lathyrus odoratus*)
5. *Clematis* species and hybrids
6. Lungwort (*Pulmonaria*)
7. Primrose (*Primula* species)
8. Perennial wallflower (*Erysimum*)
9. Spurge (*Euphorbia*)
10. *Anemone coronaria* (De Caen Group)
11. Sweet violet (*Viola odorata*)

Project: Woven plant supports

The stems of many tall perennial and annual plants may have a tendency to flop when in flower or during blustery weather. You can buy a range of supports to keep them upright, but an easy, cheaper and eco-friendly option is to make them yourself from prunings. These natural structures not only blend into the rest of the garden, offering almost invisible support when disguised by stems and foliage, they are also completely biodegradable and can be added to the compost heap when past their prime.

All you need is a few straight, sturdy stems for the uprights and flexible growth, such as willow or dogwood prunings, that can be woven around them to strengthen the support. To make a simple pyramid for sweet peas or beans, insert into the ground six sticks of the height you require, bringing them together at the top and securing them with garden twine. Weave the flexible stems in and out of the uprights to form a ring of stems, tying the ends with twine if needed. Repeat to create a

series of rings up the pyramid to make a sturdy structure.

To support tall perennials, encircle your clump of plants with a ring of flexible stems large enough to encircle your clump of plants. Then insert four straight sticks into the ring in a noughts and crosses pattern and trim off the ends. Push six upright stems of the desired height into the ground to create a circle of about the same diameter as the ring. Pop the ring over the uprights and secure it to them with twine. The flower stems will then grow through the support, which will prevent them from flopping over their neighbours.

Looking up

Sunrise and Sunset

The Spring Equinox on the 20th March marks the moment when day and night are of equal length and the beginning of astronomical/horticultural spring.

	LONDON		EDINBURGH	
	Sunrise	Sunset	Sunrise	Sunset
Fri, Mar 1	6:42:31 am	5:42:55 pm	7:00:31 am	5:49:24 pm
Sat, Mar 2	6:40:21 am	5:44:41 pm	6:58:00 am	5:51:31 pm
Sun, Mar 3	6:38:10 am	5:46:26 pm	6:55:28 am	5:53:37 pm
Mon, Mar 4	6:35:59 am	5:48:11 pm	6:52:55 am	5:55:44 pm
Tue, Mar 5	6:33:47 am	5:49:56 pm	6:50:22 am	5:57:50 pm
Wed, Mar 6	6:31:35 am	5:51:40 pm	6:47:48 am	5:59:55 pm
Thu, Mar 7	6:29:22 am	5:53:24 pm	6:45:14 am	6:02:01 pm
Fri, Mar 8	6:27:08 am	5:55:08 pm	6:42:40 am	6:04:06 pm
Sat, Mar 9	6:24:54 am	5:56:52 pm	6:40:05 am	6:06:11 pm
Sun, Mar 10	6:22:40 am	5:58:35 pm	6:37:29 am	6:08:15 pm
Mon, Mar 11	6:20:25 am	6:00:19 pm	6:34:53 am	6:10:20 pm
Tue, Mar 12	6:18:10 am	6:02:02 pm	6:32:17 am	6:12:24 pm
Wed, Mar 13	6:15:55 am	6:03:44 pm	6:29:40 am	6:14:28 pm
Thu, Mar 14	6:13:39 am	6:05:27 pm	6:27:03 am	6:16:31 pm
Fri, Mar 15	6:11:23 am	6:07:09 pm	6:24:26 am	6:18:35 pm
Sat, Mar 16	6:09:06 am	6:08:52 pm	6:21:49 am	6:20:38 pm
Sun, Mar 17	6:06:50 am	6:10:34 pm	6:19:11 am	6:22:41 pm
Mon, Mar 18	6:04:33 am	6:12:15 pm	6:16:33 am	6:24:44 pm
Tue, Mar 19	6:02:16 am	6:13:57 pm	6:13:55 am	6:26:47 pm
Wed, Mar 20	5:59:59 am	6:15:39 pm	6:11:17 am	6:28:50 pm
Thu, Mar 21	5:57:42 am	6:17:20 pm	6:08:39 am	6:30:52 pm
Fri, Mar 22	5:55:25 am	6:19:02 pm	6:06:00 am	6:32:55 pm
Sat, Mar 23	5:53:08 am	6:20:43 pm	6:03:22 am	6:34:57 pm
Sun, Mar 24	5:50:50 am	6:22:24 pm	6:00:44 am	6:36:59 pm
Mon, Mar 25	5:48:33 am	6:24:05 pm	5:58:05 am	6:39:02 pm
Tue, Mar 26	5:46:16 am	6:25:46 pm	5:55:27 am	6:41:04 pm
Wed, Mar 27	5:43:59 am	6:27:27 pm	5:52:48 am	6:43:06 pm
Thu, Mar 28	5:41:42 am	6:29:07 pm	5:50:10 am	6:45:08 pm
Fri, Mar 29	5:39:25 am	6:30:48 pm	5:47:32 am	6:47:10 pm
Sat, Mar 30	5:37:09 am	6:32:29 pm	5:44:54 am	6:49:12 pm
Sun, Mar 31	6:34:52 am	7:34:09 pm [BST begins]	6:06:16 am	7:51:14 pm [BST begins]

Moonrise and moonset

Moon Phases

◑ **THIRD QUARTER** 3 March   ◐ **FIRST QUARTER** 17 March
● **NEW MOON** 10 March   ○ **FULL MOON** 25 March

MONTH	LONDON			EDINBURGH		
	Moonrise	Moonset	Moonrise	Moonrise	Moonset	Moonrise
1	-	08:26		-	08:19	
2	00:38	08:45		01:17	08:30	
3	01:57	09:11		02:43	08:49	
4	03:12	09:51		04:06	09:21	
5	04:18	10:48		05:14	10:17	
6	05:09	12:04		06:00	11:39	
7	05:45	13:33		06:27	13:18	
8	06:10	15:08		06:44	15:02	
9	06:29	16:43		06:54	16:45	
10	06:44	18:16		07:02	18:26	
11	06:57	19:48		07:09	20:05	
12	07:10	21:19		07:15	21:44	
13	07:25	22:49		07:23	23:22	
14	07:43			07:34		
15	-	00:18	08:07	-	01:00	07:50
16	-	01:41	08:41	-	02:31	08:15
17	-	02:53	09:27	-	03:48	08:57
18	-	03:48	10:26	-	04:42	09:57
19	-	04:28	11:35	-	05:16	11:13
20	-	04:55	12:49	-	05:36	12:35
21	-	05:15	14:03	-	05:49	13:56
22	-	05:30	15:16	-	05:57	15:16
23	-	05:41	16:27	-	06:03	16:32
24	-	05:51	17:37	-	06:08	17:48
25	-	06:01	18:46	-	06:12	19:03
26	-	06:10	19:57	-	06:16	20:20
27	-	06:21	21:11	-	06:22	21:40
28	-	06:34	22:27	-	06:28	23:03
29	-	06:50	23:44	-	06:38	
30	-	07:13		00:29	06:54	
31*	02:01	08:47		02:53	08:20	

* Note: hours shift because clocks change forward 1 hour.

Average rainfall

In March, the average rainfall in the UK is 108mm (4.25in). Lower levels of precipitation and drier soils are ideal for establishing new plants, but guard against frosty nights by covering vulnerable seedlings with cloches made from glass or other recyclable or reused materials.

LOCATION	DAYS	MM	INCHES
Aberdeen	11	54	2.1
Aberystwyth	13	74	2.9
Belfast	13	71	2.8
Birmingham	10	51	2.0
Bournemouth	10	62	2.4
Bristol	10	53	2.0
Cambridge	8	33	1.3
Canterbury	7	39	1.5
Cardiff	12	85	3.3
Edinburgh	10	48	1.9
Exeter	12	112	4.4
Glasgow	14	97	3.8
Gloucester	11	51	2.0
Inverness	12	53	2.0
Ipswich	8	37	1.5
Leeds	12	77	3.0
Liverpool	11	53	2.1
London	9	43	1.7
Manchester	13	90	3.5
Newcastle upon Tyne	8	39	1.5
Norwich	9	46	1.8
Nottingham	10	45	1.8
Oxford	9	43	1.7
Sheffield	11	60	2.4
Truro	12	69	2.7

A head start with seedlings

March is the perfect time to sow many hardy seeds. They need a minimum temperature and moisture to germinate, and conditions now are usually favourable, since the soil is still wet from the winter rains and soil temperatures often rise to 6°C (43°F) or more at this time of year, which suits many seeds. Hardy crops, including broad beans, carrots, parsnips, beetroots, onions, lettuces, radishes, peas, spinach, summer cabbages, salad leaves, leeks, Swiss chard, kohlrabi, turnips and summer cauliflowers can be sown outdoors this month, especially in mild areas with light soil. However, delay sowing when heavy rain or night frosts are forecast. Remember that plants sown later in the warmer days of April often catch up earlier sowings made in poor conditions.

WHEN TO SOW

Sow your seeds at the depth specified on the packet when the soil is dry enough not to stick to your boots or tools, and it can be raked to form a level bed with a crumbly texture. Cover sowings with clear polythene or fleece to warm up the soil, which will increase germination success rates. Cloches and coldframes are a more environmentally favourable alternative to plastic sheets and do a better job as they shed rain, but they cost more initially. Fleece, cloches or frames allow sowing to be brought forward by about two weeks compared to unprotected ground.

WHICH CROPS TO COVER?

Choose crops to sow under protective covers that offer the most benefits from doing so. Try crops that need to be sown densely, such as broad beans, peas, salad onions and spinach, or those that do poorly when grown indoors and later transplanted outside – early carrots are a good example. Parsnips and maincrop carrots also resent transplanting, but can be sown later in April when the soil is warmer and they have all summer and autumn to bulk up to produce a winter harvest. It is worth sowing some beetroots and turnips under protective fleece, cloches or frames outside if you want a very early crop; while these plants don't mind being transplanted, direct sowing often results in a better crop. You can also sow more outside in April for a later harvest.

SOWING INDOORS

Lettuces, cabbages including kohlrabi, leeks and onions can be sown indoors now and then transplanted when the seedlings reach a good size. This also helps to avoid slug and snail damage, especially if you wait until your plants are a larger size and can withstand some grazing after planting out.

Transplants are also especially valuable if you have clay soil that may be too wet for seed-sowing in March; alternatively, wait until it has dried out sufficiently to sow directly, usually around mid-April.

Sweet peppers, tomatoes, cucumbers, aubergines, celery and globe artichokes can all be sown this month in a frost-free greenhouse or on a windowsill indoors. They will be at the ideal stage for planting out when the cold weather and frosts have passed.

Edible garden

Harvest your remaining winter crops now if you have any left. March can be a slow month for fresh supplies, since early-sown spring vegetables are yet to mature, although a few microgreens and young leaves grown undercover may be ready to harvest over the coming weeks.

Veg in season

FRESH SALAD LEAVES from lettuces such as corn salad grown in a greenhouse or cold frame are ready to harvest. Continue to sow more seed for a continuous crop throughout the spring and summer. **❶**

SALAD ONIONS grown undercover that are 15cm (6in) or more in height are ready to be picked now.

OVER-WINTERING BRUSSELS SPROUTS, LEEKS, PARSNIPS AND SPROUTING BROCCOLI will be cropping in March. You may still be harvesting cauliflowers, too, in mild regions. **❷**

CABBAGES grown for a winter harvest continue to provide fresh green leaves, while those sown the previous summer for a spring crop will be maturing now too. **❸**

HERBS MAY BE PUTTING ON NEW GROWTH this month, so you can start to harvest more leaves from evergreens such as bay, rosemary and sage.

Fruit in season

EARLY-CROPPING RHUBARB VARIETIES will be ready to pick at the end of the month. Harvest only from established plants; young plants will need a couple of years' growth to develop strong roots before you pick the stems. To harvest, hold the stalk at the base and gently pull it out of the ground. **❹**

ENJOY JAMS AND FROZEN RASPBERRIES that were harvested last year and frozen to bring a taste of summer to the table (see p.134).

FEELING ADVENTUROUS? The cucamelon (*Melothria scabra*) is an easy crop to grow from seed and offers something a little different to add to salads and pickles. These tiny Mexican melon-shaped fruits taste like lime-flavoured cucumbers and grow on leafy climbing plants that can be trained up a trellis or left to trail from a hanging basket. Sow the seeds indoors at the end of March or beginning of April in small pots and set out once all risk of frost has passed. Plants reach over 2.4m (8ft), but pinching out the top shoot and trimming the side shoots will keep them in check and encourage more fruits.

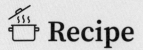 # Recipe

SPRING ONION PAD THAI

This easy stir-fry makes the most of a crop of young salad onions, as well as stored garlic and chillies. You can also add other vegetables such as carrots or sprouting broccoli, or tofu instead of prawns, depending on your preference.

INGREDIENTS

250g (8oz) pack medium rice noodle
2–3 tbsp olive or rapeseed oil
2 tsp tamarind paste
3 tbsp fish sauce
2 tsp brown sugar
1 garlic clove
1 dried chilli (optional)
3 spring onions
1 egg
200g (7oz) pack large cooked prawns
75g (2½ oz) beansprouts
Salted peanuts, chopped
Lime wedges, to serve

1 Place the noodles in a large bowl and cover with boiling water. Leave them to stand for 10 minutes until they are soft, then drain well and run under cold water until cool. Mix with a little oil to prevent them sticking together and set to one side.

2 In a bowl, mix together the tamarind paste, fish sauce and sugar. Peel and chop the garlic and finely chop the chilli, if using. Wash and cut the spring onions, including the green stems, into 1cm (½in) long pieces. Place a wok or large frying pan over a high heat and add the remaining oil. Fry the garlic, chilli and spring onions for about a minute or two until soft.

3 Push the vegetables to the sides of the wok, then crack the egg in the centre. Keep stirring until it resembles scrambled egg.

4 Stir in the prawns or tofu and beansprouts, then add the noodles. Finally, pour over the tamarind, fish sauce and sugar mixture. Fry for a couple of minutes until all the ingredients are hot, then spoon out on to warmed plates. Sprinkle some chopped peanuts over the pad thai and add wedges of lime for extra zing.

Challenges of the month

In March, the garden is coming alive with birds and bugs, most of which will promote wildlife in your garden. Gardeners can enjoy keeping a close watch on all of them, whether it's enjoying watching birds feed on bugs, or keeping a close eye on those that feed off your plants to make sure they don't cause too much damage.

SLUGS AND SNAILS will be out and about, so provide protection for vulnerable young plants and crops. Seedlings are particularly susceptible and may fare better if grown on in pots in the greenhouse or indoors until they are larger and more able to ward off attacks.

WINTER MOTHS lay their eggs between November and April, when the wingless females that emerge from pupae in the soil crawl up trunks to lay eggs on the branches of many trees, including apples, pears, plums and cherries, oaks, sycamores, hornbeams, beech, dogwoods, hawthorns, sorbus, hazels and elms. The caterpillars hatch in spring and they eat holes in the leaves and may also damage the blossom and developing fruits. The damage to ornamental trees is best tolerated, but on fruit trees you can reduce

egg-laying by placing a sticky grease band or barrier glue around the trunk and tree stake in October to trap the females. These products should be kept sticky until mid-April but they must not be strong enough to entangle other wildlife such as birds, bats or mice.

BIRDS, FROGS, AND HEDGEHOGS eat slugs, snails and vine weevils and their grubs, so encourage them in with water and safe places to hide and perch.

DAMPING-OFF DISEASE attacks seedlings, particularly those grown undercover, causing them to collapse and die. There is no cure for this soil-borne fungal disease, but you can help to prevent it by cleaning seed trays and pots thoroughly in hot water and detergent, or a mild disinfectant such as Citrox solution. Use mains water rather than water from a butt, sow thinly, and keep seedlings well ventilated.

PICK UP DISEASED LEAVES beneath roses and other plants prone to black spot to help prevent the spread of this fungal infection, which will be attacking young leaves now.

Look out for

The hare

The much-loved mad March Hare, immortalized in Lewis Carroll's 1865 book *Alice's Adventures in Wonderland*, reflects the antics of these beautiful creatures in spring, when they race around the countryside, leaping in the air, chasing one another and boxing like small, furry prize fighters. Hares can breed at any time of year, but the main season is in early spring, which is also when you may see females (jills) standing on their hind legs and boxing with overly amorous males (jacks). After mating, the young hares (leverets) are born 42–44 days later and the mother then places each one in a shallow grass-lined depression called a 'form', which she will make near a hedge, in short grass, or in a ploughed furrow.

The naturalised brown hare (*Lepus europaeus*), with its long ears and powerful hind legs, is the most abundant species in the UK, while the smaller native mountain hare (*Lepus timidus*), which has a white coat in

winter, is now restricted mainly to the Scottish Highlands. The best time to see hares is in the early morning or the evening grazing on open grassland and popping their heads up every now and again on the look-out for danger. These solitary animals spend the rest of the day in their forms, keeping a low profile. If spooked, hares will hunker down, camouflaged among the plants, but when the danger approaches, they will run off at speeds of up to 45mph, avoiding attack by outrunning their enemies and zigzagging through the fields to confuse them.

The UK hare population has declined in recent years due to a number of causes, including loss of flower-rich grassland, changes in farming practices and shooting for game.

Identifying daffodils

Daffodils (*Narcissus*) are grouped into 13 Divisions, which denote the flower shape and number of blooms on each stem. For example, the classic yellow trumpet-shaped daffodil with one flower per stem is in Division 1, while the smaller, fragrant Tazetta types are in Division 8 and have three or more blooms per stem. Division 13 is the botanical group, and includes daffodils known by their scientific names. Plant a selection of bulbs in autumn to decorate your garden and pots for a colourful display from February to May. Daffodil bulbs and plants are toxic if eaten.

NARCISSUS 'ICE FOLLIES' (DIVISION 2)
The large-cupped white blooms of this elegant daffodil age to creamy white, with one flower per stem unfurling in March.
H x S: 40 x 10cm (16 x 4in)

NARCISSUS 'ACTAEA' (DIVISION 9)
Flowering in late April, this tall poeticus daffodil features one flat-faced bloom per stem. The white flowers have a small yellow eye with red edges.
H x S: 40 x 10cm (16 x 4in)

NARCISSUS 'HAWERA' (DIVISION 5)
A triandrus daffodil with up to five lemon-yellow pendent blooms unfurling on each short stem in April and May.
H x S: 20 x 10cm (8 x 4in)

NARCISSUS 'JETFIRE' (DIVISON 6)
In March, this cyclamineus daffodil produces one clear yellow flower per stem, each with reflexed petals and an orange trumpet.
H x S: 25 x 4cm (10 x 2in)

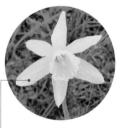

WILD DAFFODIL (*NARCISSUS PSEUDONARCISSUS*) (DIVISION 13)
Perfect for naturalizing in a wildflower garden, this dainty daffodil produces one small pale yellow flower with a darker trumpet per stem in March and April.
H x S: 35 x 10cm (14 x 4in)

NARCISSUS 'TÊTE-À-TÊTE' (DIVISION 12)
This much-loved dwarf daffodil appears as early as February, its buttercup yellow blooms with slightly darker trumpets held singly on each stem.
H x S: 15 x 5cm (6 x 2in)

Garden tales

The maidenhair tree (*Ginkgo biloba*) is one of the oldest plant species in the world, with fossils dating back to an era before the dinosaurs roamed the Earth over 290 million years ago. A native of China and common feature of our parks and roadsides today, this beautiful tree with its unusual fan-shaped foliage offers an insight into the evolution of plant species. A sole survivor of plants that appeared after ferns and before conifers, it evolved many millions of years before flowering plants. It is also known as a living fossil because there are no other plants like it: the only member of the genus *Ginkgo*, it's the only genus in the family Ginkgoaceae, which is the only family in the order Ginkgoales, and the only order in the subclass Ginkgoidae.

Maidenhair trees are dioecious, which means that the female reproductive parts are on separate trees to the male pollen-producing trees. After pollination, the tree produces seeds, which are known for their unpleasant rancid butter-like smell that's emitted as the fleshy part breaks down after it hits the soil. The tree's longevity appears to be due to its insect-resistant wood and a low incidence of disease. Six ginkgoes even survived the Hiroshima nuclear bomb, while all life around them perished, and they are still alive today. The oldest living ginkgo is thought to be 'The Li Jiawan Grand Ginkgo King' in China, which is about 3,500 years old or more.

Today, smaller and more compact cultivars of *Ginkgo*, ideal for gardens, have been introduced, while the male forms are often used as street trees, chosen for their ability to tolerate air pollution and their resilience to climate change.

Legend: The festival of Ostara

Modern-day pagans mark the spring equinox with the festival of Ostara, a celebration of the mythical goddess whose legend is said to have given rise to the association of rabbits with Easter and the tradition of giving decorated eggs.

The myths surrounding Ostara are a little blurry, however, and there is some debate about who she was and if, indeed, she was ever worshipped. Named after the Anglo-Saxon goddess Eostre, there is little written evidence about her, apart from a mention in the works of the 8th century English monk Bede. It was not until 1835, when German folklorist Jacob Grimm theorized in his book *Deutsche Mythologie* that she was a local version of a more widely known goddess, whom he named Ostara, that legends surrounding her began to spread.

A celebration of the mythical goddess whose legend is said to have given rise to the association of rabbits with Easter and the tradition of giving decorated eggs.

Some say Ostara had the head and shoulders of a hare, the creature most closely linked with the moon in mythology and with Easter; the modern-day Easter bunny evolved from legends about hares. Other myths tell a different story, in which Ostara changes a bird into a hare, for which the hare is very grateful and presents the goddess with colourful eggs. Both the hare and egg are symbols of fertility and rebirth, and have for many centuries been integral to spring and Easter celebrations. The hare's main mating season is in March and April and it is associated with fertility because it can conceive while already pregnant.

It is not surprising that eggs have also become part of the Ostara myth, since they bring forth new life, echoing the resurrection of Christ. The Celts dyed eggs red as part of their Spring Equinox celebrations to symbolize the menstrual cycle and new birth. The eggs were then buried alongside seedlings to feed the plants as they grew. It is believed that when Christianity came to Britain, the clergy wanted to discourage this pagan tradition, and encouraged children to dig up the eggs, for which they received a small gift from the priests, and the Easter egg hunt was born.

April

Traditionally a month of sunshine and showers, the garden in April is a confection of colours and hive of activity. Delicate blossoms float from the trees like confetti, while birds flit to and fro, feeding their young on a hard-won diet of insects and worms. Bright tulips join in the seasonal celebrations, their cupped blooms opening up to greet the warm sun, as spring-flowering shrubs put on their annual show of eye-catching blooms.

KEY EVENTS

Easter Monday, 1 April
Eid al-Fitr, 9 April

St George's Day, 23 April
Passover, 23–30 April

What to do

The showers traditionally associated with April are often quite brief and this month can, in fact, experience very low levels of rainfall, so keep an eye on the forecast and water if the soil is dry, paying particular attention to new trees, shrubs, and young crops planted earlier in the year. You can also sow annuals such as zinnias and cosmos indoors, and plant out early potatoes in the first week or two of April, and maincrops from mid-month (see p.94). Weeding regularly now will also pay dividends.

In the garden

PLANT EVERGREEN TREES AND SHRUBS, making sure they are at the same depth in the ground as they were in their pots or a little proud of the soil surface, with soil mounded up around the root ball. Mulch the soil with a 5cm (2in) layer of well-seasoned bark chips, leaving a gap around the stems. **1**

PRUNE EARLY SPRING-FLOWERING SHRUBS AND CLIMBERS after the blooms have faded. Well-established clematis such as *C. armandii* and *C. cirrhosa*, which are in Pruning Group 1, may not need any attention, apart from a little tidy-up if they have outgrown their space. The same applies to *C. alpina*, *C. macropetala* and *C. montana*, which bloom from April to May and are pruned in early summer. **2**

STAKE TALL PERENNIALS that may flop over their neighbours later in the season. Try making your own supports (see p.56) or buy them, encircling clumps to hold the emerging stems in place. **3**

PUT UP A BOX MOTH PHEROMONE TRAP now and another one in mid-July to trap the males. While these traps do little to reduce the damage, they warn you that breeding is about to start and the caterpillars will be hatching soon. You can then pick the pests off by hand or use a biological control. **4**

DEADHEAD DAFFODILS and other spring bulbs after the flowers have faded. Nip out the tips to allow all the plants' energies to go into building up the bulbs rather than making seed. Leave the foliage to die down naturally.

PLANT NEW AQUATICS and marginals in pond baskets filled with garden or aquatic soil, rather than compost, which is too rich in nutrients and may cause algal blooms. Check labels for the correct planting depths.

SOW OR TURF NEW LAWNS, preparing the ground before you start so that it drains freely – if you have clay soil, install drains or work plenty of sand into the top layer. Leave established lawns unmown in April to allow the flowers in them to bloom and feed pollinators.

In the fruit & veg patch

PLACE CLOCHES over young hardy crops in the garden to protect them against late frosts, which often occur in April. Cheap homemade cloches can be made using recycled clear plastic, held in place over plants with sticks or canes.

CONTINUE SOWING ANNUAL CROPS for a successional harvest. Sow tender types such as basil, cucumbers, courgettes, sweetcorn and tomatoes in pots indoors, and hardy crops such as potatoes, broad beans, lettuce, peas, spinach, salad onions, brassicas, leeks and carrots outside in the ground.

INSTALL INSECT-PROOF MESH over parsnips and brassicas to deter cabbage root fly and over your carrots to fend off carrot fly.

PRICK OUT SEEDLINGS planted earlier in the year, transplanting them into individual pots or module trays to grow on.

PLANT STRAWBERRIES outside in pots and in the ground. Runners (bare-root plants) are cheaper than pot-grown plants but will need to be planted soon after they arrive.

Indoors

WATER AND FEED LEAFY HOUSEPLANTS regularly – most will be growing more rapidly now that light levels have increased. However, take care not to overwater them, which may lead to root and stem rot, by ensuring they are in pots with drainage holes in the base and never allowing them to sit in wet compost.

WATER SUCCULENTS AND CACTI only when the compost feels bone dry, avoiding their leaves and stems if possible as you do so.

DIVIDE CONGESTED LEAFY HOUSEPLANTS whose stems sprout from the base, such as calatheas (*Goeppertia*), fiddleleaf figs (*Ficus lyrata*) and peace lilies (*Spathiphyllum*).

Plant now

1. Hardy perennials, such as *Agapanthus* **'Blue Magic'** and hostas
2. Hardy shrubs (such as *Berberis thunbergii* f. *atropurpurea* 'Rose Glow')
3. *Epimedium* species
4. *Anemonella thalictroides*
5. Deciduous viburnum (*V. carlesii* and *V. burkwoodii*)
6. Flowering currant (*Ribes sanguineum*)
7. Lilac (*Syringa* cultivars)
8. Flowering quince (*Chaenomeles* × *superba*)
9. Evergreen azaleas (*Rhododendron* species)
10. *Sorbaria sorbifolia* 'Sem'
11. Camellia (*Camellia* species and cultivars)

Project: Strawberry Tower

April is a good time to plant strawberries, and a simple, space-saving idea is to grow them in a tower of pots. Choose early, mid- and late-season strawberries to provide a succession of fruits, or opt for everbearers that produce smaller quantities of strawberries throughout the summer and early autumn.

To make the tower, you need three pots, each with drainage holes in the bottom: a large one about 50 x 45cm (20 x 18in) for the base; a smaller, shallow one for the middle; and a pot of about 20 x 20cm (8 x 8in) for the top. Frostproof terracotta pots work well, their weight helping to keep the tower stable, but you can use any containers you have to hand, as long as they have drainage holes in the base.

Fill the largest pot with peat-free multipurpose compost to about 5cm (2in) from the rim and set it on pot feet or bricks to aid drainage. Fill the second, shallow pot with the same compost, again leaving a gap between the rim and soil. Place it on the compost of the first pot, leaving an arc of exposed soil for your plants, and press down to secure it in place. Finally, fill the smallest pot with compost and set that on top of the second container, again leaving space for plants. Now add your strawberries, leaving about 10–15cm (4–6in) between the plants and positioning them so the fruits in each pot will hang down over the sides without shading those below. Water each layer, and continue to water throughout the growing season, making sure the tower is set on pot feet or bricks to allow good drainage and prevent the bottom layer becoming waterlogged.

Unless you are growing everbearers, pinch out the flowers as they appear on the plants – this allows all their energy to go into building a strong root system. You will not get strawberries from them this year, but they will produce heavier crops in the second and third years, after which they should be replaced.

Looking up

Sunrise and Sunset

As daylight hours extend, plant growth speeds up, powered by energy from the sun. Wildlife also makes use of the longer days to forage to feed their young.

	LONDON		EDINBURGH	
	Sunrise	Sunset	Sunrise	Sunset
Mon, Apr 1	6:32:36 am	7:35:50 pm	6:39:39 am	7:53:16 pm
Tue, Apr 2	6:30:20 am	7:37:31 pm	6:37:02 am	7:55:18 pm
Wed, Apr 3	6:28:04 am	7:39:11 pm	6:34:25 am	7:57:20 pm
Thu, Apr 4	6:25:49 am	7:40:52 pm	6:31:48 am	7:59:22 pm
Fri, Apr 5	6:23:34 am	7:42:32 pm	6:29:11 am	8:01:24 pm
Sat, Apr 6	6:21:20 am	7:44:13 pm	6:26:35 am	8:03:26 pm
Sun, Apr 7	6:19:06 am	7:45:53 pm	6:24:00 am	8:05:28 pm
Mon, Apr 8	6:16:52 am	7:47:34 pm	6:21:24 am	8:07:31 pm
Tue, Apr 9	6:14:39 am	7:49:15 pm	6:18:50 am	8:09:33 pm
Wed, Apr 10	6:12:26 am	7:50:55 pm	6:16:15 am	8:11:35 pm
Thu, Apr 11	6:10:14 am	7:52:36 pm	6:13:41 am	8:13:37 pm
Fri, Apr 12	6:08:03 am	7:54:16 pm	6:11:08 am	8:15:40 pm
Sat, Apr 13	6:05:52 am	7:55:57 pm	6:08:35 am	8:17:42 pm
Sun, Apr 14	6:03:42 am	7:57:37 pm	6:06:03 am	8:19:45 pm
Mon, Apr 15	6:01:33 am	7:59:18 pm	6:03:32 am	8:21:47 pm
Tue, Apr 16	5:59:24 am	8:00:58 pm	6:01:01 am	8:23:50 pm
Wed, Apr 17	5:57:16 am	8:02:39 pm	5:58:31 am	8:25:53 pm
Thu, Apr 18	5:55:09 am	8:04:20 pm	5:56:02 am	8:27:55 pm
Fri, Apr 19	5:53:03 am	8:06:00 pm	5:53:34 am	8:29:58 pm
Sat, Apr 20	5:50:57 am	8:07:40 pm	5:51:06 am	8:32:01 pm
Sun, Apr 21	5:48:53 am	8:09:21 pm	5:48:39 am	8:34:03 pm
Mon, Apr 22	5:46:49 am	8:11:01 pm	5:46:14 am	8:36:06 pm
Tue, Apr 23	5:44:47 am	8:12:41 pm	5:43:49 am	8:38:09 pm
Wed, Apr 24	5:42:46 am	8:14:22 pm	5:41:25 am	8:40:11 pm
Thu, Apr 25	5:40:45 am	8:16:01 pm	5:39:02 am	8:42:14 pm
Fri, Apr 26	5:38:46 am	8:17:41 pm	5:36:40 am	8:44:16 pm
Sat, Apr 27	5:36:48 am	8:19:21 pm	5:34:20 am	8:46:18 pm
Sun, Apr 28	5:34:51 am	8:21:01 pm	5:32:00 am	8:48:20 pm
Mon, Apr 29	5:32:56 am	8:22:40 pm	5:29:42 am	8:50:22 pm
Tue, Apr 30	5:31:01 am	8:24:19 pm	5:27:25 am	8:52:24 pm

Moonrise and moonset

Moon Phases

◑ **THIRD QUARTER** 2 April   ◐ **FIRST QUARTER** 15 April
● **NEW MOON** 8 April   ○ **FULL MOON** 24 April

MONTH	LONDON			EDINBURGH		
	Moonrise	Moonset	Moonrise	Moonrise	Moonset	Moonrise
1	03:09	09:36		04:06	09:05	
2	04:04	10:43		04:58	10:15	
3	04:44	12:05		05:30	11:45	
4	05:12	13:35		05:49	13:25	
5	05:32	15:07		06:02	15:06	
6	05:48	16:39		06:10	16:45	
7	06:02	18:10		06:17	18:24	
8	06:15	19:42		06:23	20:02	
9	06:29	21:14		06:31	21:42	
10	06:45	22:46		06:40	23:24	
11	07:06			06:53		
12	-	00:16	07:36	-	01:02	07:14
13	-	01:36	08:17	-	02:30	07:49
14	-	02:40	09:13	-	03:36	08:43
15	-	03:27	10:21	-	04:18	09:56
16	-	03:59	11:35	-	04:43	11:18
17	-	04:21	12:50	-	04:58	12:41
18	-	04:38	14:04	-	05:07	14:01
19	-	04:50	15:15	-	05:14	15:19
20	-	05:00	16:25	-	05:19	16:34
21	-	05:10	17:35	-	05:23	17:50
22	-	05:19	18:45	-	05:27	19:06
23	-	05:30	19:58	-	05:32	20:25
24	-	05:42	21:14	-	05:38	21:48
25	-	05:57	22:32	-	05:47	23:14
26	-	06:18	23:50	-	06:01	
27	-	06:48		00:40	06:23	
28	01:02	07:33		01:57	07:02	
29	02:01	08:34		02:56	08:04	
30	02:44	09:50	-	03:34	09:28	

Average rainfall

In April, the average rainfall in the UK is 70mm (2.75in), and while soil water reserves will continue to sustain most established plants in the ground, rain alone may not be sufficient for young and new plants whose roots are not long enough to tap into the moisture available at lower levels.

LOCATION	DAYS	MM	INCHES
Aberdeen	8	38	1.5
Aberystwyth	11	63	2.5
Belfast	11	60	2.4
Birmingham	10	56	2.2
Bournemouth	10	58	2.2
Bristol	10	48	1.9
Cambridge	8	38	1.5
Canterbury	8	45	1.8
Cardiff	11	72	2.8
Edinburgh	9	41	1.6
Exeter	12	94	3.7
Glasgow	12	66	2.6
Gloucester	11	69	2.7
Inverness	10	41	1.6
Ipswich	8	35	1.4
Leeds	11	66	2.6
Liverpool	10	50	2.0
London	9	50	2.0
Manchester	12	68	2.7
Newcastle upon Tyne	8	39	1.5
Norwich	9	39	1.5
Nottingham	9	48	1.9
Oxford	9	49	1.9
Sheffield	10	59	2.3
Truro	11	66	2.6

Planting for colour

There are many ways to lift the garden in spring and summer with an array of colourful plants. Tender bedding or container plants such as tobacco plants (*Nicotiana*) and petunias offer an easy and economical way to add instant colour when all risk of frost has passed.

INEXPENSIVE OPTIONS

Small plants, usually sold in cell trays before they flower, are good value and will establish better than those already in bloom – plants can flower or grow roots but seldom both simultaneously. The only downside is that these packs often include mixed colours, so if you want a particular shade, you may have to wait until they bloom or choose plants already in flower.

These young plants can also be a better environmental choice than mature potted plants, since they hold a smaller volume of potting media and use less fuel to grow and transport. The cell trays are usually made from transparent plastic which can be recycled, unlike polystyrene trays.

Cell-tray plants can be planted directly into containers or hanging baskets but are best transplanted into larger pots of peat-free compost and allowed to grow into bigger plants before being planted in beds or borders. Paper-based biodegradable pots are ideal for growing on cell-tray or small plug plants.

Plug plants are another economical choice and make growing plants such as begonias and pelargoniums, which have tiny or expensive seeds and need mollycoddling in early life, much easier. Grown in thumb-sized plugs of potting compost, these seedlings will need to be grown on into larger plants, just like cell-tray plants. Larger 'garden ready' plugs are also available, but most plugs need several weeks of growing on.

Potted bedding plants are sold in grey or taupe-coloured pots which can be recycled, too, but unlike cell-tray plants, they can be planted straight into the garden. Wait until all risk of frost has passed in late spring or early summer if your plants are not frost-hardy.

PERENNIAL FLOWER POWER

Many herbaceous perennials, such as *Echinacea* and *Penstemon*, rival bedding plants for flower abundance and, as they are reasonably hardy, you can keep them from year to year, saving the annual expense and adverse environmental consequences of buying new plants. You can save money by purchasing bare-root perennials such as peonies and hostas when the plants are dormant from late autumn to early spring. Supermarkets and other general outlets also offer a limited range of bagged plants in spring, which are competitively priced and will establish well, as long as they are fresh. Friends and other gardeners may also offer you plants, but take care they do not inadvertently bring weeds, diseases or unwanted bugs into the garden, too.

SEEDS AND BULBS

Sowing flower seeds indoors in spring or, if hardy, outdoors where they are to grow is also possible, but many plants will only attain flowering size in late summer. Exceptions include those with large seeds – nasturtiums or sunflowers, for example –or speedy hardy annuals such as calendula and California poppies. Tender cosmos and zinnias also grow quickly from indoor sowings; the young plants can then be transplanted outside after the frosts.

Also consider planting a few summer-flowering bulbs, which are cost effective and have few environmental downsides. Try acidanthera (*Gladiolus murielae*), begonias, dahlias, eucomis, freesias, galtonias, gladioli, lilies and *Triteleia laxa* for a long season of colour throughout summer and early autumn.

Edible garden

Mid-spring is known as the 'hunger gap', when winter vegetables have been harvested and most spring crops are not yet ready to pick. There are a few in season, however, so try to make the most of these.

Veg in season

LETTUCE, CHARD AND SPINACH grown in a cold frame or under cloches over winter will be ready to harvest now, while quick-maturing microgreens grown on a windowsill indoors will also deliver a few fresh salad leaves. **1**

SHRUBBY HERBS such as bay, sage, rosemary and thyme can be harvested in larger quantities as new shoots quickly replace those that have been picked. Remove the shoot tips to encourage bushier growth to develop further down the stems. **2**

ASPARAGUS CAN BE HARVESTED from mid-April to early June. This perennial crop is relatively easy to grow from bare-root plants (crowns), which should be planted in late winter or early spring. The spears are the shoots that emerge a few weeks later, but harvest only from well-established plants that are at least two years old. After harvesting for about ten weeks, leave the plants to grow on in summer, cutting the stems back in late autumn. **3**

WILD GARLIC abounds in April, filling woodlands and damp, shady areas of the garden with its sharply scented foliage

Fruit in season

MANY RHUBARB VARIETIES will be ready to harvest in April, when the pink stems topped with large leaves are growing well in the warmth and sunshine. The green part should be discarded and only the pink stems cooked and eaten.

JAMS, BOTTLED FRUIT AND FROZEN BERRIES help to plug the hunger gap at this time of year, so make sure you preserve some later in the summer and autumn when plants are laden with sweet crops.

FEELING ADVENTUROUS? The beefsteak plant (*Perilla frutescens*), also known as Shiso in Japan, is a half-hardy annual and relative of mint. Both the leaves and flowers are used in Asian dishes such as salads, fish dishes, tempura and even cocktails, adding a complex flavour that combines hints of mint, clove, cumin and citrus. Sow the seed in March or April in pots indoors and set the seedlings outside in a sunny spot when all risk of frost has passed. Plants grow to about 90 x 60cm (36 x 24in), providing plenty of leaves and flowers to harvest throughout summer and early autumn. *Perilla frutescens* var. *crispa* has pretty purple leaves.

and dainty white pompon flowers. Keep it in check in a garden by pulling up excess plants and using the leaves in salads and soups.

KALE MAY STILL BE GROWING STRONGLY now from the previous year's sowings. Try leaving the plants unharvested in early spring to provide fresh leaves and flower shoots in April when little else in available.

SPRING CABBAGES will be ready to harvest, either new plants or crops that have regrown from the stumps of those you picked earlier in the year (see p.34).

🍲 Recipe

ASPARAGUS SALAD

Make the most of the annual asparagus season, which has just begun, and freshly harvested lettuce leaves in this delicious salad. While tomatoes are not yet in season, you could replace fresh with sun-dried.

1   Heat the olive oil in a nonstick frying pan, and add the asparagus tips. Cook for 4–5 minutes, keeping them moving so that they do not burn but turn slightly brown. Add the garlic and cook for a further minute or two, then pour in 4 tablespoons of water and cook for a further minute. Remove from the heat, drain any excess moisture, and leave to cool.

2   Either boil the eggs for 5 minutes in a pan of boiling water or poach them by carefully cracking the eggs into a pan of boiling water and cooking for 2–3 minutes. Remove the eggs with a slotted spoon and set to one side.

3   Divide the salad leaves between 4 plates and top with the asparagus, tomatoes and avocado.

4   To make the dressing, place the oil, balsamic vinegar and mustard in a clean jam jar. Screw on the lid and shake until the ingredients are all well mixed. Drizzle the dressing over the salad, and serve with sliced boiled eggs or poached eggs on top.

INGREDIENTS
2 tbsp virgin olive oil
400g (14oz) asparagus tips
1 clove garlic, finely chopped
4 medium eggs
Fresh salad leaves
16 small tomatoes, halved (or sun-dried tomatoes)
1 ripe avocado, peeled and chopped

For the dressing
4 tbsp virgin olive oil
2 tbsp balsamic vinegar
1 tsp wholegrain mustard
Juice of half a lemon

Challenges of the month

Slugs and snails continue to plague young and succulent plants this month, so protect vulnerable plants with traps sunk into the soil, such as scooped out orange or melon skins. Check and empty these regularly. The soil is too cold this month for most fungal diseases to do much damage.

ADELGIDS are similar to aphids, and various species suck the sap from a range of conifers, including larch (*Larix*), spruce (*Picea*) and Scots pine (*Pinus sylvestris*). They are often covered with a white, waxy substance and may also produce galls (little round growths) on young shoots. In the case of the spruce, adelgids produce tiny pineapple-like swellings. The bugs do little damage to large trees but on smaller plants, squash or wipe them off with a tissue as soon as you see them to prevent an infestation. Encourage predators such as ladybirds, ground beetles, birds, hoverflies and earwigs into your garden.

FLEA BEETLES are tiny black beetles that feed on the leaves of all brassica crops such as cabbages, rocket, radishes and turnips, causing shot-like holes in the foliage. Seedlings are particularly vulnerable; older plants can usually survive the damage. Growing plants under fleece can prevent them from attacking your crops. Also encourage birds, ground beetles and frogs that feed on flea beetles into your garden.

CABBAGE ROOT FLY LARVAE eat the roots of cabbages, radishes and other brassicas such as swedes and turnips.

Adults look like house flies and their larvae are white maggots. To prevent the damage they cause, place a brassica collar around the base of the stems of young plants – any eggs laid on them will dry up and die. Buy or make the collars, using circles of cardboard, recycled plastic sheet or carpet underlay, about 15cm (6in) across. Alternatively, cover plants with insect-proof mesh or horticultural fleece. Crop rotation also helps reduce the problem.

GOOSEBERRY MILDEW can attack plants from late spring or early summer. Signs include powdery grey-white fungal patches on the leaves, which later turn brown, and fungus on the fruits that turns brown as they ripen. It also causes young shoots to become stunted and twisted at the top and to then die back. The fungal growths on the berries can be wiped off and the gooseberries will still be edible, but they will turn brown when cooked. To reduce mildew, prune bushes in late June or July to form an open, airy structure, and avoid fertilizing in spring with nitrogen-rich products such as poultry manure, which promote soft growth that is more vulnerable to attack – a balanced, all-purpose organic feed is a better choice.

Look out for

The hedgehog

This endearing prickly mammal has long been celebrated in children's books and folklore, and is welcomed in the garden, devouring a host of invertebrates, such as caterpillars and the occasional slug or snail, which are often all-too abundant in gardens. However, these beautiful nocturnal creatures are under serious threat, their numbers plummeting by nearly a third since 2002, with only about a million now thought to be left in the UK from a population of roughly 30 million in 1950. Gardeners are key to reversing this trend, which has been largely caused by habitat loss, the overuse of pesticides that kill their prey, and road deaths.

Our resident European hedgehogs (*Erinaceus europaeus*) are covered with about 7,000 spines, which are modified hairs that they raise up, rolling themselves into a spiky ball when danger approaches. Sadly, while this defence mechanism deters predators, it also makes them vulnerable on roads, since they freeze when threatened, rather than running.

Hedgehogs come out of hibernation in April, and you may see them scurrying around the garden at night on the hunt for a variety of insects, beetles, caterpillars, worms and birds' eggs. Making holes in boundary fences helps to extend their territory, allowing them to roam from garden to garden, while log piles covered with leaves offer them safe refuge during the day and make a cosy nest or 'hibernaculum' where they can overwinter. A garden well stocked with a variety of plants, including shrubs and tall grasses, will also provide them with cover and increase the habitat for the creatures they like to eat. Including a small pond with sloping sides in your garden will offer them easy access to a water source, too.

Identifying bluebells

Scented bluebells carpeting woodland floors up and down the country is one of April's most precious gifts. The common or native bluebell *(Hyacinthoides non-scripta)* is a much-loved wildflower, but its future was thought to be under threat from the Spanish interloper *Hyacinthoides hispanica,* which was imported during the Victorian era. The two have cross-bred to form a hybrid, *Hyacinthoides × massartiana,* which it was feared may signal the complete extinction of our native species. However, recent research shows this is unlikely, since the pollen of non-native bluebells is often misshapen, indicating lower fertility, while the common species is more fertile and sets more seeds. It's still advisable to plant only the native one and give the Spanish types and hybrids a miss. Plant the bulbs in autumn in part shade and well-drained soil that does not dry out in summer.

COMMON BLUEBELL
(HYACINTHOIDES NON-SCRIPTA)
Scented violet-blue bell-shaped flowers hang from one side of each of the curved stems, which appear among narrow, strap-shaped leaves. The common bluebell is protected under the Wildlife and Countryside Act (1981), so check where and how your supplier has sourced them.
H x S: 30 x 10cm (12 x 4in)

WHITE BLUEBELL
(HYACINTHOIDES NON-SCRIPTA 'ALBA')
The white form of the common bluebell, 'Alba' has the same slender leaves and fragrant, narrowly tubular flowers.
H x S: 30 x 10cm (12 x 4in)

ITALIAN BLUEBELL
(HYACINTHOIDES ITALICA)
This plant is not likely to hybridize with the common bluebell. It has narrow leaves and dense clusters of starry mid-blue flowers in April.
H x S: 20 x 10cm (10 x 4in)

HYBRID BLUEBELL
(HYACINTHOIDES × MASSARTIANA)
A hybrid of the common and Spanish bluebell, it is similar in appearance to the native bluebell but has flowers intermittently all around the stem.
H x S: 30 x 10cm (12 x 4in)

SPANISH BLUEBELL
(HYACINTHOIDES HISPANICA)
These plants grow more upright than the common bluebells, and the flowers develop around the stem. The strappy leaves are larger too.
H x S: 40 x 20cm (16 x 8in)

Garden tales

History: Tulip mania

The wide availability and relatively low cost of tulip bulbs makes this beautiful flower one of the most popular of all our spring plants, but there was a time when tulips cost more than gold. These beautiful blooms first arrived in the Netherlands from Turkey in the 1630s, generating huge demand for the bulbs, which were bought and sold for vast sums by wealthy traders. The Dutch at the time were enjoying a period of great prosperity and the price for some bulbs were equal to a house. Tulip sales spiked from December 1636 to February 1637 as eager investors snapped up the most prized bulbs, such as the coveted Switzer with its unusual two-tone blooms – it was later discovered that the distinctive colour breaks were actually caused by a virus.

The story of people losing their fortunes and the Dutch economy nose-diving in what was dubbed Tulip mania became legend when Scottish author Charles MacKay wrote about it in his 1841 book, *Memoirs of Extraordinary Popular Delusions and the Madness of Crowds*. However, many historians today believe that MacKay's account was wildly exaggerated and have found little evidence that the economy tanked nor that many people were made bankrupt as a result of the crash in tulip bulb prices. Nevertheless, it was a lesson that speculative bets on the direction trade prices will go is fraught with danger.

Today, while bulbs are more affordable, the Netherlands is still prospering from the sale of tulips and they remain one of the country's main exports. The flower is also celebrated every April at the famous Amsterdam Tulip Festival.

Legend: The fairy bird

One of the UK's smallest birds, the wren is a resident all year round, and can be seen in gardens, woodlands and the wider countryside. Despite its diminutive size, it has a very loud song, particularly in spring when protecting its young, which is perhaps why wrens tend to be thought of as female, hence Jenny Wren. Some also say the wren is a fairy in disguise and it was sacred to the Celtic druids, symbolizing life, energy and quick wit.

Legends also describe the wren as the king among birds, a title it won after all the birds in world gathered together for a contest to see who could fly the highest and become the sovereign. The eagle climbed the highest but as he descended, assuming victory, a small voice above him declared "I am king." The wren had tucked itself under the eagle's feathers and flew out, climbing even higher than the larger bird. The eagle and other birds pronounced it unfair that the wren had won through cunning rather than strength. They insisted on another competition, this time for the bird that swooped the lowest. Again, the wren won, this time by diving into a mouse hole. The larger birds agreed that it could be king but guarded the hole, determined to kill the wren when it came out. However, while the owl was on guard the sun momentarily blinded him and the wren took the opportunity to escape, and this is why the tiny bird still hides from eagles and hawks eager to kill it.

Harming a wren or destroying its nest is considered bad luck, too, but Early Christians did not like the bird's pagan association and declared that its loud call had betrayed Saint Stephen to his persecutors while he hid in the bushes. This legend gave rise to Wren Day, an Irish celebration held on 26 December, Saint Stephen's Day, when a wren was killed and paraded around the town on a pole by wrenboys dressed up in masks and straw suits. This tradition is still practiced in some areas today but a fake wren is now used instead of a real bird.

> Some also say the wren is a fairy in disguise and it was sacred to the Celtic druids, symbolizing life, energy and quick wit.

May

As the seasons turn from spring to summer, long hours of daylight prompt lush growth in the garden, with plants jostling for space in beds and borders. Fledglings are on the move, too, stretching their wings in preparation for flight. We also feel the energizing effects of warm sun on our faces, but for gardeners, the days never seem long enough at this busy time of year.

KEY EVENTS

May Day Bank Holiday, 6 May
Ascension Day, 9 May
RHS Malvern Spring Festival, 9–12 May
Whit Sunday, 19 May
RHS Chelsea Flower Show, 21–25 May
Spring Bank Holiday, 27 May

What to do

Temperatures in May are on the rise, rapidly drying out the top layers of soil where young plants' roots are establishing, so continue to water new trees, shrubs and perennials. Also keep deadheading spring bulbs such as tulips and camassias as soon as the flowers have faded, and prune early spring-flowering shrubs and climbers such as Clematis alpina, C. macropetala *and* C. montana *(see also p.127) if they have outgrown their space. Keep an eye out for aphids on young shoots and take action before the problem worsens (see p.105).*

In the garden

DIVIDE SPRING-FLOWERING PERENNIALS such as *Doronicum* and pulmonarias after they have bloomed. Also remove old leaves that may now be suffering from powdery mildew; the new growth that emerges later in the month should be healthy.

CUT BACK TRAILING ROCK PLANTS such as candy tuft (*Iberis sempervirens*), alyssum (*Lobularia maritima*) and aubrieta to prompt bushier growth and prevent them becoming leggy. **1**

TAKE CUTTINGS FROM TENDER PERENNIALS and shrubs that you have overwintered indoors or in a greenhouse, such as argyranthemums, pelargoniums and fuchsias. Remove 7–10cm (3–4in) shoot tips, trimming them just beneath a bud or leaf, then remove the lower leaves. Pot up the cuttings in a 50:50 mix of horticultural grit and peat-free cuttings compost, and they should take root and start producing new shoots within a few weeks. Plant outside after the frosts.

PLANT UP SUMMER CONTAINERS with half-hardy bedding or perennials, ready to be set outside when the frosts have passed at the end of May or beginning of June. **2**

TIE IN SWEET PEAS and climbing roses to their supports.

SOW SPRING-FLOWERING BIENNIALS such as forget-me-nots, wallflowers, *Bellis perennis*, and sweet williams (*Dianthus barbatus*) in pots or in shallow drills in a prepared bed outside in the garden.

REMOVE DUCK AND BLANKET WEED from ponds. Take care not to fish out tadpoles at the same time and leave the weeds on the side of the pond for a couple of days to allow any aquatic creatures trapped in them to escape back to the water.

TRY THE CHELSEA CHOP on plants such as achilleas, phlox, sedums (*Hylotelephium spectabile*) and other late-flowering perennials that can become leggy. Cut back all or some of the stems by half to keep them bushy and extend the flowering period. **3**

In the fruit & veg patch

CONTINUE SUCCESSIONAL SOWING of carrots, salad onions, lettuce, beetroots, cabbages, peas, and radishes. Sow in drills in prepared beds and thin the seedlings when they have a few leaves to the spacings recommended on the seed packs.

SOW AUTUMN CROPS such as leeks, sprouting broccoli and squash in pots or trays indoors in early May; plant out in summer.

PLANT MAINCROP POTATOES from mid-April to early May in a sunny area and prepared free-draining soil. Space the tubers about 40cm (16in) apart in trenches 12cm (5in) deep and 75cm (30in) apart. Apply a general-purpose granular organic fertilizer.

HARDEN OFF SEEDLINGS grown under cover, including climbing beans and tomatoes, that will be ready to plant out after the last frosts. Set them outside during the day for a week or two from mid to late May to acclimatize them to cooler conditions but bring them in again at night.

Indoors

PLACE TROPICAL HOUSEPLANTS on trays of damp pebbles to maintain humidity levels. Many ferns and large-leaved plants need a moist atmosphere to thrive, but they will not tolerate wet soil, so ensure yours are in pots with good drainage.

POT UP THE PLANTLETS dangling from your spider plant (*Chlorophytum comosum*), placing the base, where you may see roots emerging, into a container filled with peat-free cuttings compost. Keep moist and when new leaves start to emerge, sever the stem from the parent plant and leave the baby to grow on.

Plant now

1. Bear's breeches (*Acanthus mollis* and *A. spinosus*)
2. Granny's bonnet (*Aquilegia vulgaris*)
3. Mexican orange blossom (*Choisya* 'Aztec Pearl' AGM)
4. Foxglove (*Digitalis purpurea*)
5. Wood spurge (*Euphorbia amygdaloides* var. *robbiae*)
6. Cranesbill (*Geranium* species)
7. Sweet rocket (*Hesperis matronalis*)
8. Peony (*Paeonia*)
9. Solomon's seal (*Polygonatum* species)
10. Poppy (*Papaver* species)
11. Rhododendron (choose AGM varieties for best performance)

Project: Pollinator screen

Filling your garden with plants for pollinators is the perfect way to sustain these valuable insects throughout the year, and one way to increase the range of flowers available to them is to install a screen covered with flowering climbers. Making the most of the vertical space, this feature will not only attract a range of bees, butterflies, hoverflies and other beneficial insects, it will also enrich the garden with a wall of colour and scent.

To make the screen, start by either fixing a series of horizontal wires or a trellis panel to an existing fence or wall to support the climbing plants' twining tendrils and stems. Alternatively, if you want to create a free-standing screen to divide the garden up or mask bins or a bike shed, attach a trellis panel to two sturdy posts about 1.5m (5ft) in height, secured into the ground with metal fence post anchors. Then simply plant a range of perennial and annual climbers 30–45cm (12–18in) away from the screen and tie in the stems to the wires or trellis. Look for the RHS Perfect for Pollinators logo on plants when making your selections, but also check that the plants you choose will like your site and soil. Good options for a free-standing screen include the compact jasmine *Jasminum officinale* 'Devon Cream', *Lonicera periclymenum* 'Strawberries and Cream', the purple bell vine (*Rhodochiton atrosanguineus*) and the

annuals morning glory (*Ipomoea tricolor*) and nasturtiums (*Tropaeolum majus*).

For larger walls and fences, try the trumpet honeysuckle *Campsis radicans* in a warm, sunny spot; old man's beard (*Clematis vitalba*); and honeysuckle (*Lonicera periclymenum*). Some climbers don't even need wires or trellis to climb but, be warned, they are vigorous and will swamp a small screen. These include the climbing hydrangea *Hydrangea anomala* subsp. *petiolaris* and *Pileostegia viburnoides*; Boston ivy (*Parthenocissus tricuspidata*); and common ivy (*Hedera helix*), its autumn blooms offering overwintering insects a useful late-season food supply.

If you have space, include more than one climber to extend the flowering season, but check their pruning needs first, so that you can cut them all at the same time – untangling twining stems from different plants is difficult if they have different requirements.

Looking up

Sunrise and Sunset

The long hours of sunlight provide the energy for plants to put on a rapid rate of growth in May, while warmer nights allow them to grow unchecked by cold snaps.

	LONDON		EDINBURGH	
	Sunrise	Sunset	Sunrise	Sunset
Wed, May 1	5:29:08 am	8:25:58 pm	5:25:10 am	8:54:25 pm
Thu, May 2	5:27:17 am	8:27:36 pm	5:22:56 am	8:56:26 pm
Fri, May 3	5:25:27 am	8:29:14 pm	5:20:43 am	8:58:27 pm
Sat, May 4	5:23:38 am	8:30:52 pm	5:18:32 am	9:00:27 pm
Sun, May 5	5:21:51 am	8:32:29 pm	5:16:22 am	9:02:27 pm
Mon, May 6	5:20:05 am	8:34:06 pm	5:14:14 am	9:04:26 pm
Tue, May 7	5:18:21 am	8:35:43 pm	5:12:08 am	9:06:25 pm
Wed, May 8	5:16:39 am	8:37:18 pm	5:10:03 am	9:08:24 pm
Thu, May 9	5:14:59 am	8:38:54 pm	5:08:00 am	9:10:21 pm
Fri, May 10	5:13:20 am	8:40:28 pm	5:05:59 am	9:12:18 pm
Sat, May 11	5:11:43 am	8:42:02 pm	5:04:00 am	9:14:14 pm
Sun, May 12	5:10:08 am	8:43:36 pm	5:02:03 am	9:16:10 pm
Mon, May 13	5:08:35 am	8:45:08 pm	5:00:08 am	9:18:04 pm
Tue, May 14	5:07:04 am	8:46:40 pm	4:58:14 am	9:19:58 pm
Wed, May 15	5:05:34 am	8:48:11 pm	4:56:24 am	9:21:51 pm
Thu, May 16	5:04:07 am	8:49:40 pm	4:54:35 am	9:23:42 pm
Fri, May 17	5:02:42 am	8:51:09 pm	4:52:49 am	9:25:32 pm
Sat, May 18	5:01:20 am	8:52:37 pm	4:51:05 am	9:27:21 pm
Sun, May 19	4:59:59 am	8:54:04 pm	4:49:23 am	9:29:09 pm
Mon, May 20	4:58:41 am	8:55:29 pm	4:47:44 am	9:30:55 pm
Tue, May 21	4:57:25 am	8:56:53 pm	4:46:07 am	9:32:40 pm
Wed, May 22	4:56:11 am	8:58:16 pm	4:44:34 am	9:34:23 pm
Thu, May 23	4:55:00 am	8:59:38 pm	4:43:03 am	9:36:04 pm
Fri, May 24	4:53:51 am	9:00:58 pm	4:41:34 am	9:37:44 pm
Sat, May 25	4:52:45 am	9:02:16 pm	4:40:09 am	9:39:21 pm
Sun, May 26	4:51:41 am	9:03:33 pm	4:38:47 am	9:40:57 pm
Mon, May 27	4:50:40 am	9:04:48 pm	4:37:27 am	9:42:31 pm
Tue, May 28	4:49:42 am	9:06:02 pm	4:36:11 am	9:44:02 pm
Wed, May 29	4:48:46 am	9:07:13 pm	4:34:58 am	9:45:31 pm
Thu, May 30	4:47:53 am	9:08:23 pm	4:33:48 am	9:46:58 pm
Fri, May 31	4:47:03 am	9:09:31 pm	4:32:41 am	9:48:22 pm

Moonrise and moonset

Moon Phases

◐ **THIRD QUARTER** 1 May   ◑ **FIRST QUARTER** 15 May
● **NEW MOON** 8 May   ○ **FULL MOON** 23 May

MONTH	LONDON			EDINBURGH		
	Moonrise	Moonset	Moonrise	Moonrise	Moonset	Moonrise
1	03:15	11:16		03:56	11:02	
2	03:37	12:45		04:09	12:40	
3	03:54	14:13		04:19	14:16	
4	04:08	15:41		04:26	15:51	
5	04:20	17:09		04:32	17:27	
6	04:33	18:39		04:39	19:04	
7	04:48	20:11		04:47	20:44	
8	05:07	21:42		04:58	22:24	
9	05:32	23:09		05:14		
10	06:08			-	00:00	05:42
11	-	00:23	06:58	-	01:19	06:28
12	-	01:19	08:03	-	02:13	07:35
13	-	01:58	09:17	-	02:45	08:56
14	-	02:25	10:33	-	03:04	10:21
15	-	02:43	11:49	-	03:15	11:43
16	-	02:57	13:01	-	03:23	13:02
17	-	03:08	14:12	-	03:29	14:19
18	-	03:18	15:21	-	03:33	15:34
19	-	03:28	16:31	-	03:38	16:49
20	-	03:38	17:43	-	03:42	18:07
21	-	03:49	18:58	-	03:48	19:29
22	-	04:03	20:16	-	03:56	20:55
23	-	04:22	21:35	-	04:08	22:22
24	-	04:50	22:51	-	04:27	23:45
25	-	05:30	23:55	-	05:01	
26	-	06:26		00:51	05:56	
27	00:44	07:40		01:35	07:15	
28	01:18	09:04		02:01	08:47	
29	01:43	10:31		02:17	10:24	
30	02:00	11:58		02:27	11:59	
31	02:15	13:24		02:35	13:32	

Average rainfall

The average rainfall in the UK in May is 91mm (3.5in). However, precipitation can be very variable this month and high air temperatures will quickly dry out the top layers of soil.

LOCATION	DAYS	MM	INCHES
Aberdeen	10	54	2.1
Aberystwyth	10	62	2.4
Belfast	11	60	2.4
Birmingham	10	61	2.4
Bournemouth	8	49	1.9
Bristol	10	58	2.3
Cambridge	7	43	1.7
Canterbury	8	50	2.0
Cardiff	11	78	3.0
Edinburgh	10	48	1.9
Exeter	10	80	3.1
Glasgow	12	69	2.7
Gloucester	11	65	2.6
Inverness	11	56	2.2
Ipswich	7	39	1.5
Leeds	11	64	2.5
Liverpool	10	52	2.0
London	9	51	2.0
Manchester	11	66	2.6
Newcastle upon Tyne	9	41	1.6
Norwich	8	47	1.9
Nottingham	9	50	2.0
Oxford	10	57	2.2
Sheffield	9	54	2.1
Truro	10	58	2.3

Caring for your lawn

Grass starts to grow rapidly in May and lawns will need mowing at least once a week, ideally with an electric mower or a manual push mower if your patch is not very big. Pristine turf is seldom essential and a modest population of non-grass plants such as clovers and trefoils, for example, greatly increases a lawn's value to wildlife. Clovers are drought-resistant and fix their own nitrogen, reducing fertilizer requirements, and you can add microclover seed, specially bred for lawns, to increase the coverage. Flowers such as daisies, clover and dandelions in a lawn are important sources of nectar for pollinating insects.

Moss has a wildlife benefit and can be recycled, however, where moss is a problem, biological moss controls can be applied. These use bacterial enzymes to control the moss and work well in warming weather. They also act as mild fertilizers, keeping the grass green and growing well, while filling gaps left by the moss and helping to prevent recurrence.

Frequent mowing or using a mulching mower or mowing robot can also replace fertilizers, as the small clippings fall back into the sward where they rot down and feed the grass. Where mowings must be removed, you can compost them or use them as mulch around trees, shrubs and soft fruit.

FERTILIZERS AND FEEDING

Feeding lawns is not essential – most lawns get by without it – but it can help to produce better-quality grass. However, fertilizer is expensive and overuse can leach into the environment, so identify parts of the lawn that need feeding, such as areas of maximum wear, and only treat those.

Converting areas of lawn that are not used very much into a meadow is another way to reduce maintenance and fertilizer use. Try 'No Mow May': once you stop mowing, the taller flowering grasses and wild flowers such as clovers, hawkbit and buttercups will soon appear. Both pollinators and insect larvae such as caterpillars thrive in meadow patches. Mow your meadow again in September to prevent tussocks, and remove and compost the clippings – this will reduce the soil fertility and encourage more flowers to establish in it. Mow paths through larger swathes of meadow to provide access to enjoy the flowers and wildlife.

DEALING WITH SHADE

Shade can hinder grass growth and assessing overhanging trees now and pruning where required can make a big difference. In areas where the shade may be too deep for a lawn, consider alternatives such as evergreen groundcover plants, including Japanese spurge (*Pachysandra terminalis*) or sweet woodruff (*Galium odoratum*).

DROUGHT BUSTERS

Watering a lawn is not essential, even during summer droughts when the grass turns brown, since it will green up within a few days of rain returning. Compacted soil limits root growth and increases a lawn's susceptibility to drought, but you can reduce the problem by spiking the soil with a fork or aerating tool in spring to loosen it and allow air and rain to penetrate. If you did not do this earlier in the year, there is time to aerate grass now. Also plan for a repeat treatment in the autumn to prepare the lawn for winter rains.

Edible garden

A few fast-growing crops sown earlier in the year will be ready to harvest now, while sowing more, little and often, will help to keep supplies going throughout the summer and autumn.

Veg in season

ASPARAGUS SEASON runs from late spring to early summer; slice the tender spears just below the soil level with a sharp knife when they are ready to harvest.

RADISHES AND SALAD ONIONS are in season in May, having taken just a few weeks to mature from seed sown earlier in the spring.

LETTUCES and other hardy salad leaves grown under cloches or in containers will continue to provide fresh ingredients for salads.

YOUNG SPINACH LEAVES can be picked at the end of May from sowings made earlier in the spring. Harvesting a few leaves at a time will deliver a crop over a long period.

BABY TURNIPS sown in late winter will be ready to pick in May.

SPRING CABBAGES AND CAULIFLOWERS that were sown in the previous summer or autumn can be harvested now.

Fruit in season

THE FIRST STRAWBERRIES of the year will be ready to harvest in late May. Look for plants described as early cropping and plant in a warm, sheltered spot to guarantee fruits this month.

RHUBARB IS NOW IN SEASON and plants will be producing plenty of sweet, pink stems for pies, crumbles and fool (see p.104).

FEELING ADVENTUROUS? The New Zealand yam or oca (*Oxalis tuberosa*) is a delicious, pest- and disease-resistant root crop and can be eaten raw or cooked. Plant the little tubers directly outside in a sunny position at the end of May in shallow drills, about 8cm (3in) deep, in well-drained but fertile soil. Cover with soil and a layer of fleece if cold nights are forecast. Water plants well during dry spells, and harvest the tubers from late November when all the foliage has been frosted and died down.

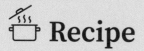 **Recipe**

RHUBARB FOOL

A traditional British dessert that was originally made with gooseberries but works equally well with rhubarb – you can substitute gooseberries when they come into season next month. It was traditionally a custard-based dessert but the whipped cream and yoghurt in this recipe give it a lighter texture. Top it with a layer of stewed rhubarb to add extra sweetness and a rich pink colour.

1 Place the rhubarb in a pan with 5 tablespoons of caster sugar. Heat gently until the stems are soft, then turn up the heat a little to allow some of the liquid to evaporate. Remove from the heat and drain over a bowl – place the captured liquid to one side.

2 Mash the stems with a fork to form a purée – don't worry if it's a bit lumpy – and add more sugar if needed. Leave to cool.

3 In a clean bowl, whip the cream until it forms soft peaks, then mix in the yoghurt. Fold in most of the cooled rhubarb, leaving some to layer on top of the fool. Chill in the refrigerator for an hour or two.

4 When cold, spoon into dishes or glasses and add a layer of the reserved purée and rhubarb juice on top. You can also sprinkle some finely chopped stem ginger over the fool to add flavour, or use a sprig of mint to garnish.

INGREDIENTS
500g (18oz) fresh rhubarb stems, chopped into small chunks
5–6 tablespoons of golden caster sugar
300ml (10 fl oz) pot of double cream
100ml (3½ fl oz) Greek yoghurt
Chopped stem ginger or sprig of mint for garnish (optional)

Challenges of the month

The usual suspects such as slugs and snails are out in force in May (see p.85), while very dry or waterlogged soils may encourage fungal diseases.

APHIDS, also known as blackfly and greenfly, suck the sap from the stems, leaves and flowers of a wide range of plants. Many also secrete a sugary honeydew, on which sooty moulds can develop, while some transmit plant viruses. Distorted growth will warn you of the presence of aphids, or you may see ants harvesting the sweet honeydew they produce. The best way to protect plants is to check tender buds of roses, honeysuckle and other susceptible plants regularly. Squash any aphids between your finger and thumb, wipe them off with a tissue or remove them with a jet of water. You can also attract aphid predators such as ground beetles, ladybirds and hoverflies by providing habitats for these insects and refraining from pesticide use.

LILY BEETLE is a bright red insect whose larvae can cause a lot of damage to lilies (*Lilium*), giant lilies (*Cardiocrinum*) and fritillaries (*Fritillaria*). While some plants seem to tolerate the beetles, others may be completely spoiled and defoliated. To keep these beetles and their larvae in check, inspect lilies and fritillaries frequently for the red beetles and pick them off as soon as you see them. Look also for their orange-red, lozenge-shaped eggs and reddish-brown larvae

on the undersides of leaves and wipe them off with a tissue. The larvae do the most damage and eat leaves, petals, stems and seedpods. Birds, frogs, wasps and ground beetles eat the larvae and sometimes the adult beetles.

APPLE SAWFLY LARVAE feed on apple fruitlets from late spring to early summer. The adult females lay eggs on the blossom and when the larvae emerge in late spring they burrow into the fruit, leaving corky trails on the skin. You may also see holes with the pest's blackish pellet-like excrement spilling out. Pick off affected fruits when you see them to prevent the larvae moving to other fruitlets or pupating in the soil when they drop. Thinning the fruits also allows more space for the pest-free apples to develop.

Look out for

The house martin

Journeying all the way from Africa, house martins (*Delichon urbicum*) begin to nest under the eaves of houses just as spring is ushering in warmer weather and delivering plentiful supplies of the insects they eat. These colourful migrants, with their blue-black and white plumage and forked tails, fly in a few weeks earlier, feeding over wetlands before returning to their traditional nesting sites. Gathering in groups of four or five pairs, they build their sturdy little nests from mud pellets and grass, lining them with feathers and vegetable fibre. A new nest takes a week or two to complete, while repairs to an existing one will be finished in a few days. These short-lived birds tend to breed for only one year, the males often returning to the nesting site from which they fledged, while the females look for new areas a few kilometres away.

House martins may have two or even three broods from May to August, laying four or five eggs each time. Both parents incubate the eggs and feed the chicks, which fledge after 22–23 days, depending on the brood size and weather. The young of the first brood often then help the parents to feed subsequent chicks, before they all leave their nesting sites in September or October to join pre-migratory flocks, in preparation for the long journey back to Africa.

Feeding exclusively on flying insects, house martins can suffer during periods of cold, wet weather when their prey is less abundant. They also feed at higher altitudes than swallows to prevent the two species competing with one another.

While we know that these little birds return to Africa each year, it's still a mystery as to exactly where they overwinter, although experts believe that they congregate over the rainforests of the Congo basin. Recent declines in populations, due to environmental changes worldwide, have placed them on the Red List, which means they are at risk.

Identifying alliums

Celebrated for their drumstick-like flowerheads, ornamental alliums make a splash from May to August. These bulbous perennials are in the same family as onions, leeks, chives and garlic, and range in colour from purple, blue and red to yellow and white. Most are well-behaved, although some, such as *Allium moly* can spread prolifically. Plant the bulbs in autumn in free-draining soil and full sun – some also take a little shade. The foliage of most alliums dies down before the flowers appear, so plant them where it will be disguised.

BLUE ALLIUM (*ALLIUM CAERULEUM*)
A beautiful species with clear blue drumstick flowerheads that appear in summer on slim stems, after the narrow mid-green leaves have faded.
H x S: 60 x 20cm (24 x 8in)

ALLIUM HOLLANDICUM
The most widely available and arguably the best of these drumstick alliums is 'Purple Sensation' AGM, which produces purple spherical flowerheads on tall, sturdy stems.
H x S: 100 x 30cm (39 x 12in)

ALLIUM CERNUUM
The delicate pink chandelier-shaped flowerheads of this compact, summer-flowering species make it stand out from the crowd.
H x S: 45 x 10cm (18 x 4in)

ROUND-HEADED LEEK (*ALLIUM SPHAEROCEPHALON* AGM)
These summer-flowering alliums have egg-shaped red-purple flowerheads opening from green buds held on slender, wiry stems.
H x S: 90 x 50cm (35 x 20in)

ALLIUM NEAPOLITANUM COWANII GROUP
One of the first alliums to bloom in April, this dainty white form looks like a swan's neck while in bud, opening to reveal loose round heads of small flowers.
H x S: 40 x 25cm (16 x 10in)

Garden tales

History: *Rhododendron ponticum* – the beauty and the beast

A visit to woods, forests or heathland along the west coast of the British Isles and Ireland in May will reveal bright pinky-purple flowers covering large swathes of the landscape. While unquestionably beautiful, *Rhododendron ponticum,* the plant responsible for these colourful blooms, provides a stark warning that not all that glitters is gold. Native to the Iberian Peninsula, Asia and China, this rhododendron was introduced to Britain in 1763 and quickly gained popularity for its large flowers and evergreen leaves, which offered shelter and privacy around country estates. Before long, it was spreading widely, and concerns were being raised as early as the mid 19th century about its invasion of the countryside.

DNA analysis of the species reveals that it is a hybrid of *R. maximum* and *R. catawbiense*, and particularly well adapted to the cool, wet conditions and acid soils found on moors and in woodlands in the UK. Spreading quickly via seed and its root systems, the plant's dense habit shades out and inhibits germination of native plants. It is also poisonous to cattle, and the nectar is harmful to bees. Even in areas where these rhododendrons have been cleared, research shows that the composition and diversity of native species takes more than 30 years to recover. This beautiful beast is also a host of the fatal sudden oak death disease (*Phytophthora ramorum*).

Listed on Schedule 9 of the UK Wildlife and Countryside Act as an invasive, non-native species, *Rhododendron ponticum* is not currently banned from sale in the UK, but the RHS and other environmental agencies are urging people not to plant it and to choose instead one of the many harmless rhododendrons with an Award of Garden Merit (AGM).

Legend: The origins of May Day celebrations

Plants and flowers have been central to May festivities since Ancient Roman times when people celebrated Floralia, the Festival of Flora, to honour the goddess of spring, flowers, and fertility. The Celts later marked the month with the Beltane festival, when they decorated their doors and windows with blossom from the hawthorn (also known as the May tree), which was associated with fertility, and lit bonfires to welcome in the new season.

From the medieval period, the first day of May was marked with feasting and dancing in towns and villages. Wood from the hawthorn tree was used to make May poles, around which the revellers sang and danced. However, while the flowers were used for garlands, they were never brought into the home since the hawthorn tree was thought to augur illness and death. The seed of this superstition may be the blossom, which was said to smell of the Great Plague – recent research shows that this could, in fact, be true since it contains the chemical trimethylamine which forms in decaying animal tissue.

In the 18th century, the figure of Jack-in-the-Green emerged as part of the May Day celebrations. Thought to have evolved from an earlier tradition where milkmaids decorated their pails and, later, their heads, with pyramids of flowers and silver objects, Jack was decked all over with leaves to resemble a tree. The character was closely associated with the chimney sweeps guild, and was often accompanied by Morris dancers, musicians, clowns and other figures. Prudish Victorians disliked the bawdy behaviour of Jack-in-the-Green and his crew, and by the late 19th century, he had all but disappeared from the festivities.

As the Jack-in-the-Green tradition was waning, the May Queen became a popular symbol of the spring celebrations. The role was played by a young girl in her early teens who was selected for her purity and dressed in white, with a crown of flowers on her head. While the idea of a goddess of flowers has its roots in Roman mythology, and Catholics celebrated May by crowning statues of the Virgin Mary with seasonal blooms, this more secular tradition is largely a Victorian invention, possibly inspired by Tennyson's popular poem 'The May Queen'. The Queen led the May Day procession, escorted by a young man and other girls with flower bouquets to 'sing in the May'.

June

Basking under the sun and refreshed by occasional showers, the June garden delivers a bounty of colourful flowers, fresh vegetables and sweet strawberries, heralding the first fruits of the season. The coolest month of the summer, June is rarely 'flaming', the phrase referring to Sir Frederic Leighton's 1895 painting of a woman sleeping in an orange dress, rather than sizzling temperatures.

KEY EVENTS
Shavuot, 12 June
Father's Day, 16 June
Eid al-Adha, 17 June
Midsummer's Day, 24 June

What to do

Plant out tender plants and crops this month and water them regularly during dry periods until their roots are established. Continue to prune late-spring flowering shrubs and sow small batches of fast-maturing crops such as lettuces and radishes for a successional harvest throughout summer and autumn. If you have let your lawn grow long in May, you can continue to let it flower into June to allow the wildflowers to self-seed, and to continue to feed pollinators.

In the garden

PLANT OUT TENDER BEDDING PLANTS that you have been growing undercover now that the frosts have passed. Remember to harden them off before setting them outside (see p.94). **1**

SOW TENDER ANNUALS such as candytuft *(Iberis)*, cosmos, satin flowers *(Clarkia)* and the poached egg plant *(Limnanthes douglasii)* in prepared beds where they are to flower for blooms later in the season. Sow away from established trees and shrubs which may cast too much shade for these plants to flower. **2**

FILL GAPS IN BORDERS with perennial plants or potted bulbs that are in bloom now, checking that they are suitable for your site and soil and will not grow too large for the space. **3**

SOW WINTER-FLOWERING PANSIES AND PRIMULAS in pots and trays undercover so that they'll be ready to plant out in the autumn. Also sow biennials, including sweet williams *(Dianthus barbatus)*, hollyhocks *(Alcea rosea)* and foxgloves *(Digitalis)*, plus perennials such as aquilegias, delphiniums and lupins indoors for flowering next year.

PLANT DROUGHT-TOLERANT SHRUBS such as rock roses *(Cistus)* and lavender *(Lavandula)* if you're able to keep them watered for a month or two during dry periods while they establish. **4**

DEADHEAD SPENT ROSE BLOOMS of repeat-flowering cultivars to encourage another flush. **5**

WEED REGULARLY, hoeing open areas of soil, removing those close to plants by hand and digging out perennial weeds to remove the whole root system. To reduce annual weed growth, cover bare soil with a mulch or a carpet of ground-covering ornamental plants such as bergenias and Japanese spurge *(Pachysandra)* in shade or rock roses *(Helianthemum)* and hardy geraniums in sunnier sites.

In the fruit & veg patch

START SOWING WINTER AND SPRING CABBAGE SEEDS undercover. Then plant the young plants of winter cabbages outside under bird- and insect-proof netting later in the summer and the spring crops in autumn.

SOW CLIMBING BEANS directly outside in early June next to their tall supports, or plant out seedlings grown undercover earlier in the year. Plant runner beans 20cm (8in) apart and French beans 25cm (10in) apart. Dwarf French French beans are best sown or planted in rows 45cm (18in) apart, allowing 15cm (6in) between plants.

PEAS, WINTER SQUASH, AND SWEETCORN can also be sown early in the month into prepared beds outside. Sow peas 7.5cm (3in) apart in a flat-bottomed trench 5cm (2in) deep and 15cm (6in) wide; plant two squash seeds per hole 1m (3ft) apart; and sow sweetcorn in a square pattern with two seeds per hole, 45cm (18in) apart. For double-sown crops, remove the weakest seedlings when they emerge.

TRANSPLANT POTTED SEEDLINGS of tender crops such as courgettes and outdoor tomatoes and cucumbers into larger containers or prepared beds outside.

Indoors

FEED SUMMER-FLOWERING HOUSEPLANTS such as African violets (*Saintpaulia*), gloxinia (*Sinningia speciosa*) and Cape primroses (*Streptocarpus*) with a fertilizer high in potassium as soon as flower buds appear. Also remove faded blooms to promote a longer display.

WATER CONSISTENTLY throughout the summer months when most houseplants are in growth, but guard against overwatering which can lead to root and stem rot. Irrigate when the top of the compost feels dry and make sure plants are in pots with drainage holes in the base to allow excess water to escape.

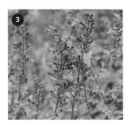

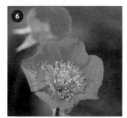

Plant now

1. Half-hardy bedding plants such as *Cosmos bipinnatus* 'Rubenza'
2. Yarrow (*Achillea millefolium*)
3. Catmint (*Nepeta × faassenii*)
4. Pinks (*Dianthus* Cherry Burst)
5. Speedwell (*Veronica* species)
6. Avens (*Geum coccineum* 'Cooky')
7. Delphinium (*Delphinium* cultivars and hybrids)
8. Sweet peas (*Lathyrus odoratus* 'Zorija Rose')
9. Pot marigold (*Calendula officinalis*)
10. Masterwort (*Astrantia major*)
11. *Wisteria floribunda* 'Kimono'

Project: Raised herb bed

Growing herbs in the garden is very easy and provides fresh leaves and flowers for the kitchen. Packed with nutrients that promote good health, the tasty foliage of many can be used in a wide range of savoury dishes, while mint (*Mentha*), fennel (*Foeniculum vulgare*) and lemon verbena (*Aloysia citrodora*) make delicious caffeine-free teas. Many herbs' nectar-rich flowers also benefit garden wildlife. Sage (*Salvia officinalis*), thyme (*Thymus*), lavender (*Lavandula*) and wild marjoram (*Origanum vulgare*) are magnets for bees and butterflies, and some seeds provide food for birds, too.

Most herbs are sun-lovers and prefer free-draining soil, so if you have sticky clay prone to waterlogging or simply want to make an attractive feature, grow them in a raised bed. Simple timber or recycled plastic frames are available as easy-to-build kits, or you can make your own by screwing together four timber planks or oak sleepers. When sourcing wood products, check that they have Forest Stewardship Council (FSC) certification, which shows that the timber is from a sustainably managed forest.

Fill the frame with a 50:50 mix of garden soil and horticultural grit – you will need less grit if using sandy soil. This will provide the perfect conditions for most Mediterranean herbs such as rosemary, thyme, sage and lavender. Other wildlife-friendly herbs include fennel, marjoram, chives (*Allium schoenoprasum*) and hyssop (*Hyssopus officinalis*). Check each plant's final height and spread, and set the tallest in the centre or where they will cast the least shade over the other herbs, with creeping plants such as thyme or trailing rosemary (*Salvia rosmarinus* Prostratus Group) around the edges. Squeeze annuals, including dill (*Anethum graveolens*) and basil (*Ocimum basilicum*), into any gaps. Leave mint out of the mix – it's best grown separately in a pot of its own where its invasive roots won't be able to smother other herbs and plants.

Looking up

Sunrise and Sunset

The summer solstice on the 20th June marks the longest day of the year. Plants use energy from the sun to grow, fuelling an abundance in the garden during this month.

	LONDON		EDINBURGH	
	Sunrise	Sunset	Sunrise	Sunset
Sat, Jun 1	4:46:16 am	9:10:37 pm	4:31:38 am	9:49:44 pm
Sun, Jun 2	4:45:32 am	9:11:41 pm	4:30:38 am	9:51:03 pm
Mon, Jun 3	4:44:50 am	9:12:42 pm	4:29:42 am	9:52:19 pm
Tue, Jun 4	4:44:11 am	9:13:41 pm	4:28:49 am	9:53:33 pm
Wed, Jun 5	4:43:36 am	9:14:38 pm	4:28:00 am	9:54:43 pm
Thu, Jun 6	4:43:03 am	9:15:33 pm	4:27:15 am	9:55:51 pm
Fri, Jun 7	4:42:33 am	9:16:25 pm	4:26:33 am	9:56:55 pm
Sat, Jun 8	4:42:07 am	9:17:15 pm	4:25:56 am	9:57:56 pm
Sun, Jun 9	4:41:43 am	9:18:02 pm	4:25:22 am	9:58:53 pm
Mon, Jun 10	4:41:23 am	9:18:47 pm	4:24:51 am	9:59:48 pm
Tue, Jun 11	4:41:05 am	9:19:29 pm	4:24:25 am	10:00:38 pm
Wed, Jun 12	4:40:51 am	9:20:08 pm	4:24:03 am	10:01:25 pm
Thu, Jun 13	4:40:40 am	9:20:44 pm	4:23:45 am	10:02:09 pm
Fri, Jun 14	4:40:32 am	9:21:18 pm	4:23:30 am	10:02:49 pm
Sat, Jun 15	4:40:27 am	9:21:48 pm	4:23:20 am	10:03:25 pm
Sun, Jun 16	4:40:25 am	9:22:16 pm	4:23:14 am	10:03:57 pm
Mon, Jun 17	4:40:26 am	9:22:41 pm	4:23:11 am	10:04:25 pm
Tue, Jun 18	4:40:31 am	9:23:03 pm	4:23:13 am	10:04:50 pm
Wed, Jun 19	4:40:38 am	9:23:21 pm	4:23:19 am	10:05:10 pm
Thu, Jun 20	4:40:49 am	9:23:37 pm	4:23:28 am	10:05:27 pm
Fri, Jun 21	4:41:02 am	9:23:50 pm	4:23:42 am	10:05:39 pm
Sat, Jun 22	4:41:19 am	9:23:59 pm	4:24:00 am	10:05:48 pm
Sun, Jun 23	4:41:38 am	9:24:06 pm	4:24:21 am	10:05:52 pm
Mon, Jun 24	4:42:00 am	9:24:09 pm	4:24:47 am	10:05:52 pm
Tue, Jun 25	4:42:26 am	9:24:09 pm	4:25:16 am	10:05:48 pm
Wed, Jun 26	4:42:54 am	9:24:06 pm	4:25:49 am	10:05:41 pm
Thu, Jun 27	4:43:25 am	9:24:00 pm	4:26:25 am	10:05:29 pm
Fri, Jun 28	4:43:59 am	9:23:50 pm	4:27:06 am	10:05:13 pm
Sat, Jun 29	4:44:35 am	9:23:38 pm	4:27:50 am	10:04:53 pm
Sun, Jun 30	4:45:15 am	9:23:22 pm	4:28:37 am	10:04:29 pm

Moonrise and moonset

Moon Phases

● **NEW MOON** 6 June   ○ **FULL MOON** 22 June
◐ **FIRST QUARTER** 14 June   ◑ **THIRD QUARTER** 28 June

MONTH	LONDON			EDINBURGH		
	Moonrise	Moonset	Moonrise	Moonrise	Moonset	Moonrise
1	02:27	14:50		02:41	15:04	
2	02:40	16:16		02:47	16:37	
3	02:53	17:44		02:55	18:13	
4	03:10	19:14		03:04	19:51	
5	03:31	20:42		03:18	21:28	
6	04:02	22:02		03:40	22:55	
7	04:45	23:06		04:17		
8	05:44	23:53		-	00:01	05:15
9	06:56			-	00:42	06:32
10	-	00:25	08:13	-	01:07	07:58
11	-	00:47	09:30	-	01:21	09:22
12	-	01:03	10:45	-	01:31	10:44
13	-	01:15	11:56	-	01:37	12:01
14	-	01:25	13:06	-	01:42	13:17
15	-	01:35	14:16	-	01:47	14:32
16	-	01:44	15:26	-	01:51	15:48
17	-	01:55	16:39	-	01:56	17:08
18	-	02:08	17:56	-	02:03	18:32
19	-	02:25	19:15	-	02:14	19:59
20	-	02:49	20:33	-	02:30	21:25
21	-	03:24	21:44	-	02:57	22:40
22	-	04:15	22:39	-	03:45	23:32
23	-	05:24	23:19	-	04:57	
24	-	06:47	23:47	00:05	06:29	
25	-	08:16		00:23	08:07	
26	00:07	09:45		00:35	09:44	
27	00:22	11:12		00:44	11:18	
28	00:35	12:37		00:50	12:50	
29	00:47	14:02		00:56	14:22	
30	01:00	15:28		01:03	15:55	

Average rainfall

As June is one of the driest months of the year, with an average rainfall of 82mm (3.2in) in the UK, annual crops and new plants and flowers will need watering regularly. Attach large water butts to downpipes to harvest as much rain as possible.

LOCATION	DAYS	MM	INCHES
Aberdeen	12	69	2.7
Aberystwyth	11	81	3.2
Belfast	11	69	2.7
Birmingham	10	68	2.7
Bournemouth	8	53	2.1
Bristol	10	56	2.2
Cambridge	9	49	1.9
Canterbury	8	45	1.8
Cardiff	10	74	2.9
Edinburgh	10	66	2.6
Exeter	9	83	3.3
Glasgow	12	68	2.7
Gloucester	10	71	2.8
Inverness	12	62	2.4
Ipswich	8	51	2.0
Leeds	11	80	3.1
Liverpool	10	64	2.5
London	9	58	2.3
Manchester	13	83	3.3
Newcastle upon Tyne	10	56	2.2
Norwich	10	63	2.5
Nottingham	10	67	2.6
Oxford	8	50	2.0
Sheffield	9	75	3.0
Truro	10	63	2.5

Front gardens

Paving front gardens is often an unfortunate necessity in towns and cities with little parking. However, this practice has damaging environmental consequences, increasing water run-off during downpours, which leads to flooding in low-lying streets and potential pollution of rivers and oceans when drainage systems become overloaded. Paving can also increase the localized temperatures on hot days, so make sure to consider your choice of materials thoughtfully.

Both heavy rain events and heatwaves are forecast to increase because of climate change, but the unwanted effects of these events can be mitigated by laying porous paving materials over soil and including plants in your garden. You could even add small trees such as crab apples and flowering cherries to corners not needed for parking, where they could potentially cool your property by shading it in summer and reduce wind speed in winter after the leaves have fallen. However, trees can cause subsidence on some clay soils, so grow shrubs instead, if this is a potential problem. Whatever your soil type, you can use climbers including *Clematis alpina* and shade-loving *Hydrangea anomola* subsp. *petiolaris* to scale vertical surfaces, and hedges instead of fences and walls to define your boundaries.

POROUS SURFACES
Gravel is a cost-effective, porous material, ideal for front gardens. Plant spring bulbs, hardy geraniums, heucheras, ornamental grasses and other tough plants through the gravel, and also consider planting strips that will sometimes be covered by a parked car, avoiding the areas immediately under the wheels. Low-growing *Ajuga reptans*, cotoneasters, ivies and thymes are good choices for parking spots.

Low-maintenance options include low-growing evergreens such as euonymus, *Mahonia aquifolium* and *Juniperus*

squamata 'Blue Carpet'. Dry shade near the house walls is challenging, but *Bergenia* and *Epimedium* are charming and very robust options for these sites. Variegated shrubs, including euonymus and sedges such *Carex oshimensis* 'Evergold', add colour in places where flowers may be difficult to grow.

INCREASE YOUR WELLBEING

RHS research has found evidence that plants in front gardens enhance people's sense of wellbeing, when compared to unplanted spaces. Where there is no room for planting in the ground, you can use container-grown plants such as *Choisya* and lavender – ideally maintain them with water from butts attached to the downpipes from the roof. Plants grown in pots will need more care and attention than those in the ground, but suit even the tiniest front garden.

Vegetation, especially evergreen plants, has also been shown to capture urban atmospheric pollution. The leaves of hedges provide very large surface areas and make efficient pollution traps while also helping to reduce noise pollution. Hedges also offer cover and nesting sites for wildlife, and food for birds if they produce berries. Pyracantha and *Cotoneaster franchetii* are reliable sources of berries, the latter being notable for its ability to reduce pollution. Other wildlife-friendly plants include catmint (*Nepeta*) and sedum (*Hylotelephium*) for sunny areas and honeysuckle (*Lonicera*) for walls and fences.

Edible garden

In June, you can reap the rewards of crops sown last autumn or earlier in the year. Remember that picking fruits and pods regularly will, in many cases, encourage a longer and more bountiful harvest.

Veg in season

LETTUCE AND ORIENTAL GREENS continue to provide fresh salad leaves in early summer, along with radishes, beetroots and salad onions that have been sown in batches throughout spring. **❶**

PEAS SOWN DIRECTLY INTO THE GROUND in March will be bearing the first seed pods this month. Pick them when the pods are young and the peas tender. Also sow more now for a September harvest. **❷**

THE LAST OF THE SPRING CABBAGES will be ready to harvest early this month, while new sowings can be made in June, July or August for crops next year.

AUTUMN-SOWN BROAD BEANS will be delivering a crop of tender crops in June. Harvest them when young, before you can see the beans swelling inside the pods. Freeze any that you cannot use straight away.

Fruit in season

GOOSEBERRIES MAY NOT BE QUITE RIPE in June but some berries can be harvested this month for making jam, pies and tarts. Leave the remaining fruits to ripen and eat these fresh in July and August.

BLACK, RED AND WHITECURRANTS will start to fruit in June. Use your fingers to gently pull the stems, known as 'strigs', from the bushes. Plants will produce fruits for a few weeks, so harvest them regularly. **❸**

FEELING ADVENTUROUS? Daikon or mooli (*Raphanus sativus* var. *longipinnatus*) is a long, white radish with a mild peppery flavour, which can be eaten raw in salads, roasted, boiled or steamed like a carrot, or used for making pickles. The leaves can also be cooked and eaten as a green vegetable. It is quick and easy to grow; sow the seeds in late June in moisture-retentive soil and full sun, then thin seedlings to 20cm (8in) spacings. Cover crops with fleece to prevent attacks from cabbage root fly and flea beetle. The 30cm (12in) roots will be ready to harvest in about six weeks. **❹**

🍲 Recipe

STRAWBERRY FLAN

Freshly picked strawberries are the star of this delicious dessert.

1   Sift the plain flour into a bowl, add the diced butter and rub between your fingertips until the mixture resembles fine breadcrumbs. Add the milk or water, 1 tablespoon at a time, until the mixture forms a dough. Cover with a clean cloth and chill in the refrigerator for 20–30 minutes. Roll out the pastry on a floured surface to make a circle large enough to cover the base and sides of a deep, 23cm (9in) fluted, loose-bottomed tart tin. Trim the excess and prick the base with a fork. Place back in the refrigerator.

2   To make the crème pâtissière, pour the milk into a pan with the vanilla pod. Bring to a simmer, then turn off the heat. In a large bowl, whisk the yolks and sugar for 10 minutes until fluffy, then add the flour and whisk lightly for a minute or two. Remove the vanilla pod and pour the warm milk slowly into the egg mixture while whisking. Clean the pan, then pour the mixture back in and gently bring to the boil, stirring until it thickens. Take the pan off the heat, cover with baking paper and leave to cool.

3   Preheat the oven to 180°C (160°F/Gas 4). Remove the pastry case from the fridge, cover with baking paper and add baking beans or rice on top. Place on a baking tray and blind-bake for 15 minutes. Remove the beans/rice and paper, then cook for a further 10–15 minutes until golden. Leave to cool, then transfer to a wire rack.

4   When cold, spoon the crème pâtissière on to the base, then place the strawberries in circles on top. Warm the jelly in a pan with 2 tablespoons of water until melted. Brush over the strawberries and leave for a couple of minutes to set before serving.

INGREDIENTS

250g (8oz) plain flour
125g (4oz) cold butter, diced
1–3 tbsp milk or water
Baking beans or rice
500g (1lb) small strawberries, hulled and halved
4 tbsp redcurrant jelly or apricot jam

For the crème pâtissière
350ml (12 fl oz) whole milk
1 vanilla pod, split lengthways
4 large free-range egg yolks
100g (4oz) golden caster sugar
25g (1oz) plain flour
Finely grated zest of 1 lemon

Challenges of the month

Aphid attacks peak this month, their attentions generally focused on tender buds and young crops in the first instance. Check plants regularly and remove them, following the advice on page 105.

CAPSID BUGS are small flying insects that cause brown-edged holes in the shoot tips of the leaves of many types of plants, including apples, beans, potatoes and flowers, which may fail to open. The two types that damage plants are the brightly coloured common green capsid (*Lygocoris pabulinus*), and the tarnished or bishop bug (*Lygus rugulipennis*) which is a mottled brown colour. The apple capsid (*Plesiocoris rugicollis*) also feeds on young fruitlets, causing bumps or raised corky growths to develop on the mature apples and pears, but the taste of the fruits is unaffected.

Removing dead vegetation in late winter helps destroy overwintering sites for the tarnished capsid bug. Also encourage the pest's natural predators such as birds, hedgehogs and ground beetles.

CABBAGE CATERPILLARS, the larvae of the cabbage white butterfly and cabbage moth, feed on cabbages, turnips, swedes and other brassicas, as well as nasturtiums, and can completely defoliate these plants. The easiest way to control them is to cover vulnerable crops with insect-proof mesh netting, making sure it does not touch the plants. Inspect plants and wipe off any yellow butterfly eggs and round white

moth eggs. Biological controls are available too.

RUSTS are a group of fungal diseases that attack a wide range of plants, from trees and shrubs to herbaceous perennials and annuals. Rust causes pale spots on the foliage that develop into raised pustules on the lower surface of the leaves, which may then turn yellow and fall off. Heavy infections can reduce the vigour of a plant but rust is rarely fatal, except in the case of antirrhinum rust. To reduce the incidence of the disease, avoid fertilizers high in nitrogen, which promotes soft leaf growth vulnerable to attack. In autumn and winter, also remove diseased and dead leaves from the ground (do not compost them) to prevent the spores overwintering and reinfecting plants the following year.

Look out for

The urban fox

The first sightings of red foxes (*Vulpes vulpes*) living in urban areas were in the 1930s and since then populations have grown and it's now possible to spot them searching for food or playing on the lawn in many domestic gardens across the UK.

The fox's success is due to its ability to adapt to a wide range of habitats and foods. Part of the Canidae family, along with wolves and domestic dogs, rural foxes have a diet that consists of about 95 per cent meat, while those in urban settings eat a more varied diet of fruit, vegetables, household scraps, insects, birds and small mammals such as rats and mice, thereby helping to keep rodent pest numbers under control.

The piercing screams you may hear on January nights are the females (vixens) calling out to attract a male (dog), and not cries of pain during mating. In March, the female finds a sheltered spot under a shed or hedge to deliver her litter of four or five cubs or kits. The young will stay with her for a few weeks before emerging in April, when they can often be seen playing in the garden.

Foxes are highly skilled at sourcing a plentiful supply of provisions, and you will rarely see a malnourished animal. A survey by a UK charity, The Fox Project, found that none of the 15,000 adult foxes it rescued was starving.

While these alluring creatures rarely come into direct contact with humans, they will view guinea pigs and rabbits as easy prey, so ensure your pets are secure in their hutches at night. Bear in mind that an adult fox can squeeze through a 10cm (4in) hole and easily scale a 2m (6ft 6in) fence, so you cannot deter them very easily if they wish to pay your garden a visit.

Identifying clematis

Clematis are prized for their twining stems of colourful flowers which can be used to decorate a variety of vertical surfaces. By combining different types, you can also enjoy flowers or decorative seedheads throughout the year, beginning with the winter- and early-spring flowering species such as *C. cirrhosa* and *C. alpina,* through to the summer-flowering hybrids, and finally those that put on a show in autumn, such as the viticella clematis, with their smaller blooms, and the golden nodding bells of *C. tangutica.* Look out for those with an Award of Garden Merit (AGM) for the best of the bunch.

CLEMATIS REHDERIANA AGM
Flowering from late summer to early autumn, the masses of scented pale yellow bells look spectacular dancing on slim stems on a sunny wall or fence.
H x S: 6 x 2.5m (20 x 8ft)

CLEMATIS MONTANA
This large species flowers from late spring, with simple, often scented white or pink blooms. It is ideal for climbing through a tree or over a shed or large wall.
H x S: 10 x 4m (33 x 13ft)

CLEMATIS 'PRINCESS DIANA' AGM
Small trumpet-shaped pink flowers adorn this compact clematis from late summer to mid-autumn. Like the viticella clematis, this texensis variety is generally disease-free.
H x S: 2.5 x 1m (8 x 3ft)

CLEMATIS CIRRHOSA VAR. *PURPURASCENS* 'FRECKLES' AGM
A winter-flowering evergreen clematis, 'Freckles' sports bell-shaped cream flowers with reddish-brown spots and dark green leaves.
H x S: 4 x 1.5m (13 x 5ft)

CLEMATIS 'ARABELLA' AGM
A compact, long-flowering clematis, perfect for growing in a large pot over a tripod frame, it produces dainty mauve-blue flowers from midsummer to autumn.
H x S: 1.8 x 1m (6 x 3ft)

Garden tales

History: When is a geranium a pelargonium?

While these plants are a mainstay of summer bedding displays, many people still use the common name geranium for what is actually a pelargonium. Confusion between the two plants dates back to the 18th century when the Swedish botanist Carl Linnaeus grouped the hardy geranium, a beautiful border plant, and the tender pelargonium into one genus which he called *Geranium*. Both plants belong to the same plant family, Geraniaceae, but in 1789 Charles Louis L'Héritier de Brutelle discovered that they were two separate genera and named the tender one *Pelargonium*.

The name is derived from the Greek *pelargós*, which means 'stork' and refers to the seedheads which resemble a stork's beak. However, this only blurred the distinction between the two even further, since the other common name for a hardy geranium is crane's bill, so named because its seedheads also resemble a bird's beak.

Today, there are many different types of pelargonium to choose from, including the shrubby Regal and more compact

Angel types, as well as the Zonal plants that have a dark band on their leaves. Trailing pelargoniums are useful for edging containers, their stems of ivy-like leaves providing a foil for the dainty blooms. The group of scented-leaf pelargoniums are also crowd-pleasers and include plants that smell of roses, eucalyptus, mint, lemon, orange, balsam or apple, their perfume released when you brush against them or touch the foliage. Some pelargoniums will survive a few degrees of frost, but in most parts of the country, they are best overwintered indoors to bloom the following year.

Legend: Summer solstice superstitions

A magical time of year when the sun is furthest away from the equator, the summer solstice is associated with many ancient myths and traditions. The day has been celebrated since the Neolithic era, over 6000 years ago, when Stonehenge in Wiltshire was created as a monument to the sun's power and aligned towards the sunrise on the summer solstice.

In Neolithic cultures in Northern and Central Europe, people marked the day by lighting bonfires which they believed would increase the sun's strength, boosting the growth of their crops and delivering a good harvest. Bonfires were also lit and jumped over to ward off demons and bring good luck to lovers.

In parts of Scandinavia, the longest day offers up to 24 hours of sunlight, which the Vikings would use to hunt, settle disputes and conduct raids on other tribes.

> As late as the 19th century, the solstice was believed to be a magical day when spirits and fairies could contact humans.

Christians were keen to distance themselves from pagan traditions and combined solstice celebrations with St John's Day (24 June), which commemorated St John the Baptist and is now also known as Midsummer's Day. People wore garlands of flowers to ward off the devil and baptisms of children who had died as pagans were acted out on this special day. The 'chase devil', known today as St John's wort (*Hypericum*) because of its association with the holy day, was thought to be a particularly powerful antidote to any evil brewing within the community. As late as the 19th century, the solstice was believed to be a magical day when spirits and fairies could contact humans.

Many people continue to celebrate the summer solstice today, and thousands flock to Stonehenge to see the sun rise between the standing stones. In other Northern Europe countries, the tradition of lighting bonfires also continues, while girls wear flowers in their hair and homes are decorated with garlands of flowers and foliage. In some parts of Scandinavia, people dance around a pole on Midsummer's Day in a festival similar to the May Day celebrations in the UK.

July

The long, hot days in July allow us time to slow down a little and enjoy the abundance of flowers, vegetables and fruits that summer brings. As we potter around the garden watering and deadheading to the sound of birdsong, with the sweet fragrance of honeysuckle and jasmine filling the air, these simple chores relax and renew us, melting away the stresses of the day.

KEY EVENTS
RHS Hampton Court Palace Garden Festival, 2–7 July
Battle of the Boyne, 12 July
St Swithin's Day, 15 July
RHS Flower Show Tatton Park, 17–21 July

What to do

Keeping the garden tidy, productive and beautiful are the main jobs for July. Deadheading spent flowers, particularly those of roses, will keep plants flowering for longer. There may also be containers and crops that need to be kept watered. Consider installing a drip hose attached to a timer to make efficient use of water – it will also water your plants for you while you're on holiday. Mowing the lawn and removing weeds are other ongoing tasks. Try to dig out weeds before they flower or set seed.

In the garden

DIVIDE BEARDED AND OTHER RHIZOMATOUS IRISES Bearded iris can become congested after a few years. To reinvigorate plants, divide the rhizomes (knobbly root-like structures) about six weeks after flowering ❶. Dig up the clump carefully and, with a knife, carefully remove the healthy, younger rhizomes, together with the leaves, around the edge ❷. Compost old or shrivelled sections. Trim the leaves of each rhizome section to 15cm (6in) ❸. Replant in groups of three to five, 15–30cm (6–12in) apart, ensuring the top half of the rhizome is above the soil surface, or buried just below it on light sandy soils ❹.

CLEAN AND TOP UP BIRD BATHS REGULARLY with fresh water from the tap. Keep water features and ponds topped up, too. When pond levels are low, use rainwater from a butt or, if using tap water, leave it for about 24 hours to allow the chlorine to dissipate before adding it.

LEAVE YELLOW LAWNS UNWATERED; they will soon green up again without any irrigation when rain returns.

LIGHTLY CUT BACK LAVENDER to remove the spent flowers, which will help to keep the plants bushy and productive.

In the fruit & veg patch

SOW AUTUMN AND WINTER SALAD LEAVES such as lambs' lettuce, rocket, mizuna and mibuna and pak choi.

CONTINUE SOWING FRENCH BEANS until the end of the month for a late-season crop (see p.114 for planting tips).

CONTINUE TO SOW SPRING CABBAGES for fresh greens next year. Remember to cover your crops with insect-proof netting to protect them from cabbage white butterflies and moths.

REMOVE THE STEM TIPS of outdoor cordon tomatoes once they have made four trusses of flowers, taking them back to one leaf beyond the top truss. Bush and trailing tomatoes can be left unpruned. Keep the compost or soil consistently moist as the fruits develop to prevent them from splitting, and feed plants every 10 days to two weeks with a high potash liquid organic fertilizer.

PINCH OUT THE TOPS OF RUNNER BEANS when they reach the top of their supports. This encourages bushier growth on the lower stems and allows the plant to put more of its energy into making pods.

FREEZE SUMMER FRUITS such as raspberries and gooseberries. Spread the fruits on a baking tray, freeze them, and then bag them up and return to the freezer.

Indoors

ASK A FRIEND TO WATER your houseplants when you're on holiday, or, if no one is available, fill your sink with water and set them out in their pots on a wet towel on the draining board. Place one end of the towel in the water, and it will then draw up moisture, which the plants will be able to access through the holes in the bottom of their pots.

DEADHEAD FLOWERS AS THEY FADE and remove any blooms that fall on the compost, which could start to rot on the damp surface and spread fungal diseases. The same practice can be carried out outdoors with repeat-flowering roses (see below).

Plant now

1. Half-hardy annuals (such as *Zinnia elegans* 'Queeny Orange')
2. Water lilies (*Nymphaea*)
3. Penstemon (*Penstemon*)
4. Phlox (*Phlox*)
5. Alstroemeria (*Alstroemeria*)
6. Verbascum (*Verbascum*)
7. Black-eyed susan (*Rudbeckia*)
8. Coneflower (*Echinacea*)
9. Hardy geraniums (*Geranium*)
10. Daylily (*Hemerocallis*)
11. Montbretia (*Crocosmia*)

Project: Mini wildlife pond

Attract a whole host of wildlife to your garden by creating a small pond. It can be almost any size but if you have space, create one about 1m (3ft) deep in the centre with sloping edges, which will keep a reservoir frost-free in winter and allow birds, hedgehogs and other creatures easy access, without falling in.

To make a pond, you will need some old carpet or proprietary pond underlay and butyl pond liner to make the feature watertight. Also check that you don't have a high water table, which will push up the liner, by digging a test hole. If you hit water, move the location of the pond, or make a shallower feature.

First mark out your pond – use a length of hosepipe as a guide for a smooth curved edge – and dig out a hole. Create a shelf around the edges about 45cm (18in) deep and 30cm (12in) wide, and make a gentle slope up to the soil surface along at least one edge of the pond. Then dig out a central area about 75cm (30in) deep and a final section of 1m (3ft), to create two steps from the surface to the base. Use a spirit level laid over a plank of wood to check that all sides of the pond are level.

Remove any large and sharp stones in the walls and base and lay the underlay or carpet over the surface, smoothing it out as much as possible. Centre the liner over the hole and push down in the middle, pleating it along the sides of the steps. Fill the centre with water to keep the liner in place. Continue to pleat the liner over the sides and top, then fill the pond to the surface with water. When full, trim the butyl liner, leaving about 30–45cm (12–18in) around the edges, which you can cover with soil and plants, or rocks and stones, to disguise it. Leave the water for a day or two for the chlorine to dissipate before adding marginal plants around the edges and a waterlily in the centre, planting each in a pond basket and aquatic compost.

Looking up

Sunrise and Sunset

Long days and short nights provide the perfect conditions for rapid plant growth. The intense sunlight also dries out the soil, so keep checking for signs of drought stress.

	LONDON		EDINBURGH	
	Sunrise	Sunset	Sunrise	Sunset
Mon, Jul 1	4:45:57 am	9:23:03 pm	4:29:28 am	10:04:01 pm
Tue, Jul 2	4:46:41 am	9:22:42 pm	4:30:23 am	10:03:29 pm
Wed, Jul 3	4:47:28 am	9:22:17 pm	4:31:20 am	10:02:54 pm
Thu, Jul 4	4:48:17 am	9:21:48 pm	4:32:21 am	10:02:14 pm
Fri, Jul 5	4:49:09 am	9:21:17 pm	4:33:25 am	10:01:31 pm
Sat, Jul 6	4:50:03 am	9:20:43 pm	4:34:32 am	10:00:43 pm
Sun, Jul 7	4:51:00 am	9:20:06 pm	4:35:42 am	9:59:53 pm
Mon, Jul 8	4:51:58 am	9:19:26 pm	4:36:55 am	9:58:58 pm
Tue, Jul 9	4:52:59 am	9:18:43 pm	4:38:10 am	9:58:00 pm
Wed, Jul 10	4:54:02 am	9:17:56 pm	4:39:29 am	9:56:59 pm
Thu, Jul 11	4:55:06 am	9:17:08 pm	4:40:49 am	9:55:54 pm
Fri, Jul 12	4:56:13 am	9:16:16 pm	4:42:13 am	9:54:46 pm
Sat, Jul 13	4:57:22 am	9:15:21 pm	4:43:38 am	9:53:34 pm
Sun, Jul 14	4:58:32 am	9:14:24 pm	4:45:06 am	9:52:19 pm
Mon, Jul 15	4:59:44 am	9:13:24 pm	4:46:36 am	9:51:01 pm
Tue, Jul 16	5:00:57 am	9:12:21 pm	4:48:08 am	9:49:40 pm
Wed, Jul 17	5:02:13 am	9:11:16 pm	4:49:42 am	9:48:16 pm
Thu, Jul 18	5:03:29 am	9:10:08 pm	4:51:18 am	9:46:49 pm
Fri, Jul 19	5:04:47 am	9:08:58 pm	4:52:55 am	9:45:19 pm
Sat, Jul 20	5:06:07 am	9:07:45 pm	4:54:34 am	9:43:47 pm
Sun, Jul 21	45:07:27 am	9:06:30 pm	4:56:15 am	9:42:11 pm
Mon, Jul 22	5:08:49 am	9:05:12 pm	4:57:58 am	9:40:33 pm
Tue, Jul 23	5:10:12 am	9:03:52 pm	4:59:41 am	9:38:53 pm
Wed, Jul 24	5:11:37 am	9:02:30 pm	5:01:26 am	9:37:10 pm
Thu, Jul 25	5:13:02 am	9:01:06 pm	5:03:13 am	9:35:24 pm
Fri, Jul 26	5:14:28 am	8:59:39 pm	5:05:00 am	9:33:36 pm
Sat, Jul 27	5:15:55 am	8:58:11 pm	5:06:49 am	9:31:46 pm
Sun, Jul 28	5:17:23 am	8:56:40 pm	5:08:38 am	9:29:54 pm
Mon, Jul 29	5:18:52 am	8:55:07 pm	5:10:28 am	9:27:59 pm
Tue, Jul 30	5:20:21 am	8:53:32 pm	5:12:20 am	9:26:03 pm
Wed, Jul 31	5:21:51 am	8:51:56 pm	5:14:12 am	9:24:04 pm

Moonrise and moonset

Moon Phases

● **NEW MOON** 5 July   ○ **FULL MOON** 21 July
◐ **FIRST QUARTER** 13 July   ◑ **THIRD QUARTER** 28 July

MONTH	LONDON			EDINBURGH		
	Moonrise	Moonset	Moonrise	Moonrise	Moonset	Moonrise
1	01:15	16:55		01:11	17:30	
2	01:34	18:22		01:23	19:06	
3	02:00	19:44		01:41	20:36	
4	02:38	20:54		02:11	21:49	
5	03:30	21:47		03:01	22:39	
6	04:37	22:24		04:11	23:09	
7	05:53	22:49		05:34	23:27	
8	07:11	23:07		07:00	23:38	
9	08:27	23:21		08:24	23:45	
10	09:40	23:32		09:43	23:51	
11	10:51	23:42		11:00	23:55	
12	12:01	23:51		12:15		
13	13:10			-	00:00	13:30
14	-	00:01	14:22	-	00:05	14:47
15	-	00:13	15:36	-	00:11	16:09
16	-	00:28	16:53	-	00:19	17:34
17	-	00:48	18:12	-	00:32	19:00
18	-	01:17	19:26	-	00:53	20:21
19	-	02:01	20:29	-	01:31	21:24
20	-	03:03	21:15	-	02:33	22:05
21	-	04:22	21:48	-	04:00	22:28
22	-	05:52	22:11	-	05:39	22:43
23	-	07:24	22:28	-	07:20	22:52
24	-	08:55	22:42	-	08:58	22:59
25	-	10:23	22:54	-	10:33	23:05
26	-	11:49	23:07	-	12:07	23:12
27	-	13:16	23:21	-	13:40	23:19
28	-	14:43	23:39	-	15:15	23:30
29	-	16:10		-	16:51	23:45
30	00:02	17:33		-	18:22	
31	00:35	18:46		00:10	19:41	

Average rainfall

July is one of the driest months of the year – the average UK rainfall is 94mm (3.7in). Mature plants can usually withstand summer drought, unless they're growing in a pot, but remember that vegetable crops will need regular irrigation in dry weather.

LOCATION	DAYS	MM	INCHES
Aberdeen	12	71	2.8
Aberystwyth	13	86	3.4
Belfast	13	74	2.9
Birmingham	10	66	2.6
Bournemouth	8	50	2.0
Bristol	10	59	2.3
Cambridge	8	48	1.9
Canterbury	7	43	1.7
Cardiff	11	84	3.3
Edinburgh	11	72	2.8
Exeter	9	74	2.9
Glasgow	13	83	3.3
Gloucester	11	71	2.8
Inverness	11	62	2.4
Ipswich	9	49	1.9
Leeds	11	75	3.0
Liverpool	11	65	2.6
London	8	50	2.0
Manchester	13	97	3.8
Newcastle upon Tyne	10	52	2.0
Norwich	9	57	2.2
Nottingham	9	65	2.6
Oxford	8	53	2.1
Sheffield	9	62	2.4
Truro	11	71	2.8

Preserving water

Water shortages are frequent in the UK due to high demand from domestic and industrial users. In dry summers, usage can exceed supply, resulting in excessive water extraction from rivers, which in turn causes environmental damage, particularly to wetlands.

During droughts, water companies may also introduce restrictions such as hosepipe bans. Watering by hand with buckets and cans is unlikely to lead to excessive use but sprinklers, and incorrectly calibrated drip irrigation and hosepipes, particularly if you leave them unattended, use large volumes of water and can be very wasteful.

Gardeners can reduce their use of mains water by planting and managing their gardens carefully. For example, lawns turn brown if left unwatered in dry periods but soon green up once rain returns. Sunny, dry plots suit Mediterranean-type plants such as *Ceanothus*, *Cistus*, *Cytisus*, lavenders, rosemary, salvias and thymes, and when used in conjunction with ornamental grasses, spring bulbs and autumn cyclamen, they make highly attractive low-water plantings.

PRIORITIZING YOUNG TREES
Established trees and shrubs obtain sufficient moisture from deep in the soil to survive very dry summers, although they may shed their leaves. Newly planted trees and shrubs, however, are very vulnerable to drought-stress for their first two years until the root system becomes more extensive. Give these priority and water as often as every three days in very dry weather. Tree irrigation watering bags placed next to the trunks and filled with water that slowly seeps out to keep roots moist are effective and use supplies economically.

WATERING VEGETABLES

Vegetables need regular watering for a good crop, but savings can be made by considering their physiology. For example, peas and beans need watering only at flowering time – watering earlier produces more leaves but not more pods. Leafy vegetables such as lettuce and cauliflower ideally need watering through their lives, but during droughts a good soak at the earliest 'rosette' stage does nearly as much good as watering more regularly.

EFFICIENT WATERING

Watering the soil close to plants, using a 'bund' or low wall of soil around a plant, if necessary, to retain the water, is better than spraying moisture over the stems and leaves. Similarly, a thorough soak from time to time is more effective than little and often. As much as four watering cans per square metre (1.2 sq yd) may be needed to thoroughly wet the root zone. Containers are especially thirsty, but larger pots filled with loam-based compost and grouped together will be more water-efficient than smaller pots. Mediterranean-type plants are very good choices for containers in sunny spots.

Collecting rainwater in water butts works well in an ordinary summer, but they will soon empty during prolonged droughts, limiting their contribution at these critical times. If you have an extensive roof area and the space in your garden, large tanks, possibly underground, have more potential. Tanks can be costly, and buried storage tanks will need a pump to get the water out, but surplus IBC stackable industrial containers can be an economical option where appearance doesn't matter.

Edible garden

As well as the bountiful harvests below, crops such as peas, salad leaves, radishes, and beetroots will be ready to pick or pull throughout the month, if you sowed the seed in batches every few weeks in spring.

Veg in season

CARROTS sown in early spring will produce sweet young roots in July. **1**

NEW POTATOES will be ready to harvest from chitted tubers planted in midspring. Plant more tubers now for an autumn feast.

ONIONS, SHALLOTS AND GARLIC planted the previous autumn or in early spring will be ready to harvest. Lift the bulbs on a sunny day and leave them on the ground to dry out before storing.

BEANS, INCLUDING BROAD, FRENCH AND RUNNER beans, as well as peas and mangetout, will be ready for picking throughout July.

BROCCOLI AND SPINACH provide 'greens' in midsummer from crops sown earlier in the year.

CHILLI PLANTS grown in pots in a greenhouse or warm sunny spot outside will start to produce their spicy fruits.

CUCUMBERS AND COURGETTES start to crop in July; pick them regularly for a continuous crop.

SMALL TOMATOES start to ripen in midsummer; you may have to wait until August for larger fruits.

Fruit in season

CHERRIES ripen on the trees now, so pick them before they fall to the ground or the birds steal the lot. ❷

SUMMER-FRUITING RASPBERRIES are ripe for picking in July. Freeze or make jam with any gluts (see p.134).

GOOSEBERRIES are now sweet and juicy, ideal for cooking with or without sugar, depending on your taste. ❸

MIDSEASON STRAWBERRIES ripen in July, making the perfect low-calorie snack. ❹

FEELING ADVENTUROUS? The 'Marina Di Chioggia' pumpkin is a real show-stopper, the fruits resembling warty green aliens that have landed in the garden when they mature in autumn. The flesh is rich and meaty, and can be roasted, baked or steamed. Soak the seed overnight and sow under cover in spring or directly outside in a prepared bed from late May to early July, watering plants well. Feed every 14 days with a potassium-rich organic fertilizer and lift the developing fruits on to a piece of wood or upturned terracotta pot to ripen. Pick fruits before the first frosts; they can be stored indoors for up to six months.

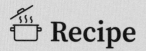 **Recipe**

SPINACH AND COURGETTE LASAGNE

This delicious lasagne is quick and easy to make and combines July's fresh crops of spinach, courgettes, onions and garlic.

1   Lightly steam the spinach for a minute or two until wilted, then leave to cool and squeeze out any excess liquid.

2   Heat the oil in a frying pan over a medium heat, add the garlic, onion and sliced courgettes and cook for a couple of minutes until soft. Then add the ricotta, spinach, half the cream and half the parmesan, mixing well. Season and set to one side.

3   Heat the oven to 180°C (350°F/Gas 4). Spread a third of the filling over the base of a 20 x 30cm (8 x 12in) baking dish, cover with 3 lasagne sheets, then add a layer of sliced courgettes. Repeat twice more, then add the remaining cream on the top, finishing off with a layer of parmesan. Bake for 20 minutes if using pre-boiled pasta sheets or 40–45 minutes for fresh pasta. Serve with a green salad.

INGREDIENTS

500g (18oz) spinach
1 tbsp olive oil
2 garlic cloves, crushed
I onion, finely chopped
4–5 courgettes (sliced)
250g (8oz) tub of ricotta
100ml (3 fl oz) double cream
100g (3½oz) grated parmesan
9 fresh lasagne sheets (or pre-boil dry sheets for 5 minutes)

Challenges of the month

This month, make sure to protect your crops from birds, caterpillars and small insect herbivores. Water regularly during dry spells to prevent powdery mildew (white fungal disease) from developing on your plants.

GLASSHOUSE WHITEFLY is a small white sap-feeding flying insect and its creamy-white scale-like nymphs feed mainly on indoor and greenhouse plants, such as tomatoes, peppers and cucumbers. The flies excrete a sticky substance (honeydew), which also promotes the growth of sooty moulds. You can spot the pests on plants and the adults will fly up when disturbed. Whitefly sometimes affects outdoor plants during very hot summers too. The best way to keep numbers down is to use a biological control of tiny parasitoid wasps (*Encarsia formosa*) that infect the nymphs.

BLOSSOM END ROT causes dark blotches on the ends of fruiting vegetables such as aubergines, tomatoes and peppers, which can then become sunken and flattened. It is caused by a lack of calcium in the fruits; the soil or compost is unlikely to be deficient in this mineral, but poor or erratic water supplies that carry it through the plant can mean that it doesn't reach the fruits. Make sure the soil is consistently moist around the roots by watering daily or even twice a day in hot weather. Covering the soil or compost with a mulch (layer) of organic matter will also help to conserve soil moisture.

POTATO BLIGHT is a serious fungal disease that spreads rapidly through the foliage and tubers of potatoes in warm, wet weather. A few potato varieties show some resistance to the disease, and early-cropping types are less likely to succumb, since the disease increases as summer progresses. The first signs are rotting leaves that shrivel and turn brown; you may also notice a white fungal growth on the underside of the foliage. Brown lesions may develop on the stems, after which the tubers turn reddish-brown and soft as the rot spreads. Dispose of affected material by burying it deeply in the ground, below root level, or take it to the local council recycling facility. Do not compost it.

There is no cure for blight, but mounding up the soil around the stems can help to prevent the fungal spores washing down into the soil from affected leaves or stems to infect the tubers below. Cut the stems of diseased plants down to the ground and remove, then dig up the tubers about two weeks later when their skins have hardened; they should be disease-free and edible. Also remove and destroy all potatoes left in the soil after harvesting and rotate your crops to reduce the risk of potential reinfection from soil-borne spores.

Look out for

The painted lady butterfly

A migrant butterfly to the UK, the arrival of the painted lady (*Vanessa cardui*) in summer offers another reason to celebrate this bountiful season. Its distinctive orange-brown wings with black and white markings make the painted lady easy to identify, and the spiny black caterpillars with a yellow stripe down each side can be seen on many wild and cultivated plants a few weeks after the adults arrive.

This little butterfly's amazing migration patterns and stamina make it truly remarkable. Research shows that this super-powered species makes an incredible 9,000 mile round trip from tropical Africa to the Arctic Circle, although we now understand that a single butterfly will fly only part of the way and the whole journey is undertaken by a few consecutive generations. After the first leg of the journey, a butterfly will lay its green eggs on suitable plant material, and the adults that metamorphose from the caterpillars then continue the epic journey north or south, depending on the season.

Unlike another butterfly migrant, the clouded yellow (*Colias croceus*), which flies in from Africa and southern Europe but then usually settles to breed in the south of the country, the whole population of painted ladies keeps moving from Africa to northern Europe and back again through this intergenerational series of breeding and migrating. None overwinter in the colder countries such as the UK.

Radar records show that painted ladies fly at an average altitude of over 500 metres, way beyond the gaze of the naked eye at ground level. Travelling at speeds of up to 30mph and helped by favourable thermals and dry conditions, they move swiftly north in spring and summer, and return south in the autumn and winter.

According to Butterfly Conservation, while many butterfly populations are in decline, numbers of painted ladies are steady or increasing slightly, perhaps boosted by higher temperatures due to climate change.

Identifying roses

Different types of roses offer something for everyone, whatever your garden size or situation. The categories include hybrid teas, with strong stems each topped with one large flower; the bushier floribundas, which produce clusters of flowers on each stem and bloom throughout the season; and the compact polyanthas, with their clusters of small flowers that appear through summer and autumn. For tiny spaces, try compact patio roses, which produce clusters of small blooms over a long period. Ramblers have tall climbing stems, and clusters of small flowers, usually produced in one flush in summer, while climbers tend to be less vigorous and bear larger flowers that appear throughout the season. Also check labels for roses with fragrant flowers.

ROSA CHANDOS BEAUTY AGM
An elegant hybrid tea rose with highly scented cream flowers with a hint of apricot that repeat bloom through summer and autumn.
H x S: 90 x 75cm (36 x 30in)

ROSA 'ALEXANDRE GIRAULT'
A large rambling rose with arching stems of glossy, dark green foliage and clusters of fully double, highly fragrant, rose-pink blooms in early summer.
H x S: 5 x 3.5m (16 x 12ft)

ROSA SUNSEEKER AGM
A compact, glossy-leaved patio rose that produces clusters of small, slightly fragrant, reddish-orange flowers from summer to mid-autumn.
H x S: 45 x 60cm (18 x 24in)

ROSA FASCINATION AGM
A bushy floribunda rose, with dark green, glossy foliage and lightly fragrant pale pink flowers that appear throughout summer and autumn.
H x S: 1 x 1m (3 x 3ft)

ROSA 'COMPASSION' AGM
A vigorous climbing rose with glossy dark green foliage on red stems, and fragrant, double, pink-tinged coppery-apricot flowers from summer to mid-autumn.
H x S: 3.5 x 3.5m (12 x 12ft)

Garden tales

History: Fairchild's mule, the first plant hybrid

We now take for granted the millions of hybrid plants and flowers available to grow in our gardens or on our allotments, but the science behind hybridization was unknown until the early 18th century when a nurseryman from Hoxton in London discovered that plants had sexual organs and could be cross bred.

That nurseryman was Thomas Fairchild and he had developed his City Gardens business on what was then a centre of market gardening a few miles east of the capital. By the early 1700s he had gained a reputation for his rare flowers and fruit plants – he was one of the first to grow a banana plant in Britain and had a vineyard with over 50 grape varieties. At the time, little was known about the way in which plants reproduced and the idea that new varieties could be developed without God's intervention was considered sacrilegious, when most people believed in creationism.

However, Fairchild was curious about the oddities that appeared in gardens and the wild when plants cross-bred naturally, and he experimented to see if he could produce one artificially. Success came in 1717 when he produced the first-ever hybrid by crossing a carnation pink (*Dianthus caryophyllus*) with a sweet william (*Dianthus barbatus*) to produce *Dianthus caryophyllus barbatus*. The plant became known as Fairchild's Mule, a first-generation sterile *Dianthus* hybrid, and set in motion a new era of research into plant hybridization.

Legend: The owl – wicked yet wise

Flying silently under the cover of night with large eyes piercing the darkness, the owl is famously associated with wisdom and knowledge, but in some mythologies and cultures this beautiful bird is also regarded as an omen, a malevolent creature that augurs death.

In Ancient Greek myths, the owl was sacred to Athena, the Goddess of Wisdom, who carried the bird on her shoulder. It advised her of hidden meanings and lit up her blind side, enabling her to speak the whole truth, rather than a half truth. Similarly, in Roman mythology, the bird is the emblem of Minerva, the Goddess of Wisdom.

The owl was also revered in Celtic folklore, where it was considered sacred, with magical powers to see into the future, echoing its ability to see in the dark and swivel its head around to view the world from all angles. The owl's reputation for wisdom is based on this seemingly supernatural perception and ability to root out deceit. In Welsh mythology, the Goddess Arianrhod shapeshifted into an owl, which empowered her to see into the darkness of the human soul. She moved swiftly through the night, her wings of comfort and healing giving solace to those who sought her help.

In Christian and Jewish mythology, the bird is associated with Lilith, variously described as the mother of Adam's demonic offspring or his wife before Eve. Although not mentioned in the Torah, folklore says she was banished from Eden for her disobedience to Adam and portrayed with owl's wings and taloned feet.

In many cultures, the owl is believed to be a portent of death or bad luck. Its haunting calls are thought to presage death, and seeing a bird during the day is believed to be a particularly bad omen. The owl is also a messenger, bringing news through dreams or meditation.

Today, some of these myths and legends persist in popular literature. Owl in the *Winnie the Pooh* stories is described as wise and advises on important matters, while in the Harry Potter books, owls are the messengers, flying between the magical and muggle world.

August

Flower seeds rattling in their pods like mini maracas while apples colour up on the trees, ripening under the late summer sun, remind us of nature's gifts and new life yet to come. Returning from holiday, we may also discover the resilience of many plants in the garden that sail on without pampering, parched perhaps but reviving again when rain returns.

KEY EVENTS

Bank Holiday in Scotland, 5 August
RHS Rosemoor Flower Show, 16–18 August
Janmashtami (*Hindu festival*), 26 August
Summer Bank Holiday, 26 August

What to do

Continue to water young plants and those in containers, while also deadheading the spent flowers of roses, annuals, and perennials such as penstemons, nepeta and dahlias that will repeat flower. Also save seed from favourite flowers and fruits, but be aware some seed may not come true, reverting to the look and habit of the original species. Longer grass can help lawns to withstand drought, so mow less often and raise the cutting height on the mower to its maximum level. Also leave the clippings in situ to act as a mulch between the blades of grass to help preserve soil moisture.

In the garden

PRUNE RAMBLING ROSES after flowering if you can reach the stems, taking out dead and diseased growth and cutting back old flower stems to reinvigorate plants. Stems out of reach will still flower the following year if left uncut.

CUT BACK GERANIUMS and other early summer-flowering perennials that have bloomed, including astrantias, nepetas and *Alchemilla mollis*. This reduces self-seeding and encourages fresh foliage to develop, with perhaps a few sprays of flowers later. **❶**

GROUP CONTAINERS in a shady spot and water well before going on holiday. Setting them on a shallow tray of water will help to keep them hydrated for a week or two. **❷**

TAKE CUTTINGS FROM EVERGREEN SHRUBS such as *Artemisia, Ceanothus, Cistus, Erica,* and *Hebe*. Remove a non-flowering stem of 10–15cm (4–6in) in length, cutting just below a leaf. Remove the lower leaves and soft tips, retaining about four leaves. Insert the base of the cutting into a pot filled with a 50:50 mix of peat-free compost and horticultural grit. Water well and cover the pots with clear plastic held away from the foliage with small sticks, then leave in a shaded greenhouse or warm area, keeping the compost moist. When the cuttings have rooted you will notice new growth developing from the stems, at which point remove the clear plastic. Keep cuttings undercover until spring.

HARVEST SEED FROM ANNUALS AND PERENNIALS on fine, dry days when the seedpods have turned brown and you can hear the seeds rattling inside. Remove the pods and break them open over a paper envelope. Discard any debris and store in a cool dry place to sow in autumn (if hardy) or the following spring. **❸**

In the fruit & veg patch

SOW SEEDS OF SALAD ROCKET, mustard and other leaves for a crop in autumn. Lettuce will not germinate if temperatures are too high, but sowing in late afternoon can help, as the cooler nights overcome this dormancy.

CUT DOWN THE FRUITING CANES OF SUMMER RASPBERRIES to the base after they have cropped, and tie in six to eight strong new canes that have developed this year, which will bear fruit next year.

WATER AND FEED TOMATO PLANTS regularly throughout August, removing any yellow or diseased leaves promptly.

HARVEST BEANS REGULARLY and freeze any excess. Pick the beans when young and tender, which will also help to encourage more to form. Use the beans inside tough older pods in stews and casseroles, boiling them well to soften them up.

CONTINUE TO LIFT AND DRY ONIONS AND GARLIC on dry days (see p.142).

Indoors

MOVE HOUSEPLANTS away from strong sun in summer, as it may scorch their leaves and lead to poor growth. Even cacti and succulents can become bleached under strong sunlight, but they need good light for the rest of the year so remember to move them back into a brighter position as autumn progresses.

HUMIDITY LEVELS MAY BE LOWER IN SUMMER so open the windows to allow more moisture in, move them into a shadier spot, and set their pots on trays of damp pebbles to increase atmospheric moisture.

MOVE PLANTS OUTSIDE for a few weeks while night temperatures remain high, checking first that your plants are in pots with drainage holes in the base and placing them in light shade at first to acclimatize them. The extra sunlight and humidity in the garden will help to boost their growth.

Plant now

1. Japanese anemone (*Anemone × hybrida*)
2. Bedding chrysanthemums (*Chrysanthemum* cultivars)
3. Dahlia (*Dahlia*)
4. Fortune saxifrage (*Saxifraga fortunei* AGM)
5. Shasta daisy (*Leucanthemum × superbum*)
6. Angel's fishing rods (*Dierama pulcherrimum*)
7. Autumn crocuses (*Crocus speciosus* and *Colchicum autumnale*, such as **'Album'**)
8. Michaelmas daisy (*Symphyotrichum* species)
9. Aster (*Eurybia × herveyi*)
10. Sedum (*Hylotelephium spectabile* AGM)
11. Bistort (*Persicaria amplexicaulis*)

Project: Succulent bowl

If you're in need of extra late-summer colour for a patio or terrace, a container filled with drought-tolerant succulents is an easy, low-maintenance option. Choose a selection of hardy plants, such as houseleeks (*Sempervivum*), which look like tiny cacti and come in a wide range of colours; and low-growing sedums such as *Sedum acre*, *S. spathulifolium* and *S. sieboldii*. Or, if you plan to set the bowl outside only during the summer months, you could also include houseplants such as agaves, echeverias, aloes and haworthias, which will be happy in a sunny, sheltered spot in the garden, but must be brought inside when temperatures fall in early autumn.

To make your succulent display, select a low, wide terracotta or glazed bowl with drainage holes at the bottom. Add a 50:50 mix of peat-free potting compost and horticultural grit, filling the bowl up to about 2.5cm (1in) below the rim. Water your plants before planting them in the bowl, checking they are set at the same level in the compost as they were in their original pots. Firm the compost around them, then water and leave to drain. Finally, add a layer of gravel over the compost surface and set your bowl

in a sunny, sheltered spot. Make sure that water can drain from the base by placing it on some stones, gravel or pot feet to lift it off the ground. During a normal British summer these plants will need watering no more than once every two weeks, or less if rain has fallen during that time.

If you planted hardy species and are leaving the bowl outside all year, set it close to the house or a wall where the bowl will be protected from heavy rain – these succulents can tolerate low temperatures but not soggy soil. Adding a biological control for vine weevil in August or September will help protect plants against this root-munching insect, too.

Looking up

Sunrise and Sunset

The light intensity in August is starting to decline, slowing growth, but many plants bloom now while bees and other pollinators are still flying.

	LONDON		EDINBURGH	
	Sunrise	Sunset	Sunrise	Sunset
Thu, Aug 1	5:23:22 am	8:50:17 pm	5:16:05 am	9:22:04 pm
Fri, Aug 2	5:24:53 am	8:48:37 pm	5:17:58 am	9:20:01 pm
Sat, Aug 3	5:26:25 am	8:46:55 pm	5:19:52 am	9:17:57 pm
Sun, Aug 4	5:27:58 am	8:45:11 pm	5:21:47 am	9:15:51 pm
Mon, Aug 5	5:29:31 am	8:43:26 pm	5:23:42 am	9:13:44 pm
Tue, Aug 6	5:31:04 am	8:41:39 pm	5:25:38 am	9:11:34 pm
Wed, Aug 7	5:32:38 am	8:39:51 pm	5:27:34 am	9:09:23 pm
Thu, Aug 8	5:34:12 am	8:38:00 pm	5:29:30 am	9:07:11 pm
Fri, Aug 9	5:35:46 am	8:36:09 pm	5:31:27 am	9:04:57 pm
Sat, Aug 10	5:37:21 am	8:34:16 pm	5:33:24 am	9:02:42 pm
Sun, Aug 11	5:38:55 am	8:32:22 pm	5:35:21 am	9:00:25 pm
Mon, Aug 12	5:40:31 am	8:30:26 pm	5:37:18 am	8:58:07 pm
Tue, Aug 13	5:42:06 am	8:28:29 pm	5:39:16 am	8:55:48 pm
Wed, Aug 14	5:43:41 am	8:26:31 pm	5:41:14 am	8:53:27 pm
Thu, Aug 15	5:45:17 am	8:24:31 pm	5:43:11 am	8:51:06 pm
Fri, Aug 16	5:46:52 am	8:22:31 pm	5:45:09 am	8:48:43 pm
Sat, Aug 17	5:48:28 am	8:20:29 pm	5:47:07 am	8:46:19 pm
Sun, Aug 18	5:50:04 am	8:18:26 pm	5:49:05 am	8:43:54 pm
Mon, Aug 19	5:51:40 am	8:16:23 pm	5:51:03 am	8:41:28 pm
Tue, Aug 20	5:53:16 am	8:14:18 pm	5:53:01 am	8:39:01 pm
Wed, Aug 21	5:54:52 am	8:12:12 pm	5:54:59 am	8:36:34 pm
Thu, Aug 22	5:56:28 am	8:10:05 pm	5:56:57 am	8:34:05 pm
Fri, Aug 23	5:58:03 am	8:07:58 pm	5:58:55 am	8:31:36 pm
Sat, Aug 24	5:59:39 am	8:05:49 pm	6:00:52 am	8:29:05 pm
Sun, Aug 25	6:01:15 am	8:03:40 pm	6:02:50 am	8:26:34 pm
Mon, Aug 26	6:02:51 am	8:01:30 pm	6:04:48 am	8:24:03 pm
Tue, Aug 27	6:04:27 am	7:59:19 pm	6:06:45 am	8:21:30 pm
Wed, Aug 28	6:06:03 am	7:57:08 pm	6:08:43 am	8:18:57 pm
Thu, Aug 29	6:07:39 am	7:54:56 pm	6:10:40 am	8:16:23 pm
Fri, Aug 30	6:09:15 am	7:52:43 pm	6:12:38 am	8:13:49 pm
Sat, Aug 31	6:10:50 am	7:50:30 pm	6:14:35 am	8:11:14 pm

Moonrise and moonset

Moon Phases

● **NEW MOON** 4 August　　○ **FULL MOON** 19 August
◑ **FIRST QUARTER** 12 August　　◐ **THIRD QUARTER** 26 August

MONTH	LONDON			EDINBURGH		
	Moonrise	Moonset	Moonrise	Moonrise	Moonset	Moonrise
1	01:22	19:43		00:52	20:37	
2	02:23	20:24		01:55	21:12	
3	03:36	20:53		03:15	21:33	
4	04:54	21:13		04:40	21:46	
5	06:11	21:28		06:05	21:54	
6	07:25	21:39		07:26	22:00	
7	08:37	21:49		08:44	22:05	
8	09:47	21:59		09:59	22:09	
9	10:56	22:08		11:14	22:13	
10	12:07	22:19		12:30	22:19	
11	13:19	22:32		13:49	22:25	
12	14:34	22:49		15:11	22:36	
13	15:51	23:13		16:37	22:52	
14	17:07	23:49		18:00	23:21	
15	18:14			19:11		
16	-	00:41	19:07	-	00:10	20:01
17	-	01:53	19:46	-	01:26	20:31
18	-	03:19	20:13	-	03:01	20:48
19	-	04:52	20:32	-	04:43	21:00
20	-	06:25	20:47	-	06:25	21:08
21	-	07:57	21:00	-	08:05	21:14
22	-	09:27	21:13	-	09:42	21:21
23	-	10:57	21:27	-	11:19	21:28
24	-	12:26	21:43	-	12:57	21:37
25	-	13:56	22:05	-	14:35	21:50
26	-	15:22	22:35	-	16:10	22:12
27	-	16:39	23:17	-	17:34	22:48
28	-	17:42		-	18:37	23:45
29	00:15	18:27		-	19:17	
30	01:24	18:58		01:00	19:41	
31	02:40	19:20		02:24	19:55	

Average rainfall

Although the 20-year average rainfall for the UK in August is 117mm (4.6in), in many areas, this is often the driest month of the year and water evaporates quickly from the soil surface, so ensure your pots and young plants are well irrigated.

LOCATION	DAYS	MM	INCHES
Aberdeen	11	68	2.7
Aberystwyth	13	86	3.4
Belfast	14	85	3.3
Birmingham	10	68	2.7
Bournemouth	8	60	2.4
Bristol	11	75	3.0
Cambridge	9	56	2.2
Canterbury	8	57	2.2
Cardiff	12	105	4.1
Edinburgh	10	72	2.8
Exeter	11	92	3.6
Glasgow	14	95	3.7
Gloucester	11	72	2.8
Inverness	12	65	2.6
Ipswich	8	48	1.9
Leeds	13	86	3.4
Liverpool	12	72	2.8
London	9	68	2.7
Manchester	15	100	3.9
Newcastle upon Tyne	10	64	2.5
Norwich	9	66	2.6
Nottingham	10	64	2.5
Oxford	9	62	2.4
Sheffield	10	65	2.5
Truro	12	71	2.8

Hardy tropicals

Hardy plants with a tropical or jungly look that can survive winters in sheltered gardens with well-drained soils in southern England and other mild areas create a colourful jungle effect during high summer.

Plants that require no winter protection should do the heavy lifting in these schemes to limit the amount of care you will have to provide each year. However, as some are not hardy to very low temperatures, be prepared to replace frosted plants if a very cold winter strikes.

HEIGHT AND STRUCTURE

Achieve the look with robust small trees including the palm-like *Cordyline indivisa*, true hardy palms such as *Chamaerops humilis* (dwarf fan palm) and the fleshy-leaved evergreens *Eriobotrya japonica* (loquat) and hardy eucalyptus. Tree ferns can also be used to add height to a tropical scheme. Another option is to use hardy trees that you cut back hard each spring (coppice), which regrow vigorously and produce huge leaves. These include *Catalpa speciosa, Liriodendron chinense* and, most remarkable of all, *Paulownia tomentosa.*

Shrubs that look tropical but are quite hardy include *Abutilon*, with its colourful bell-like flowers; *Fatsia japonica*, which has big hand-shaped leaves; the similar *Trochodendron aralioides*; and *Tetrapanax papyrifer,* with its tall stems of large spreading leaves.

Spiky swordlike foliage suits this look, too. Consider the silvery *Astelia chathamica*; *Beschorneria yuccoides*, with its huge flower spikes; and *Phormium tenax*, which comes in many colours and is resistant to wind damage in blustery sites such as by the coast.

FLOWERS AND FOLIAGE

Plants that swiftly grow tall flowering spikes from large rootstocks and tubers in the summer warmth include

Despite their stature, bananas are also herbaceous perennials, and some, notably *Musa basjoo*, will survive outdoors over winter if protected from the rain and cold. This is done by erecting a cylinder of chicken wire, lined with fleece or hessian, generously enclosing the plant. Once in place, fill the cage with straw and place a recycled plastic sheet on top to shed rain.

begonias, cannas, dahlias and the marvel of Peru (*Mirabilis jalapa*). Purple-leaved cultivars of cannas and dahlias will also add spots of colour. In dry soils these can be left to overwinter beneath a generous mulch of bark chips. Elsewhere, lift and store begonia, canna and dahlia tubers in a frost-free shed or garage. These plants also need a moist, fertile soil for the best results. Herbaceous plants suited to exotic gardens include ferns and big-leaved hostas for shade and agapanthus, fuchsia, *Lobelia cardinalis* and *L. tupa* in sunny areas.

CLIMBING HIGH
Tender annual climbers such as *Ipomoea lobata*, *I. tricolor* ' 'Heavenly Blue', nasturtiums, *Rhodochiton atrosanguineus* and *Thunbergia alata* require moist fertile soil to put on their spectacular shows. With the exception of the nasturtiums, these are best bought as small plants in spring so they attain their desired height and flower during the summer and early autumn. Hardy passion flowers also look particularly dramatic and although often cut back to ground level in winter they usually quickly regrow in spring.

Edible garden

Continue harvesting cucumbers, peas, beans, carrots, and potatoes, which started to crop in July. Herbs provide fresh leaves from spring but tender types such as basil, dill and coriander are also available to harvest now.

Veg in season

TOMATOES ARE IN SEASON in August, as the fruits ripen quickly under the warm summer sun. Harvest daily and make sauces or purées with any gluts.

AUBERGINES IN A GREENHOUSE or on a windowsill should offer a crop now, if the weather has been warm.

PEPPERS AND CHILLIES grown in the greenhouse or on a sunny patio will ripen as the month progresses.

SUMMER SQUASHES including courgettes are ready to harvest in August. Pick frequently to encourage more flowers and fruits. Also continue to harvest cucumbers.

SWEETCORN IS READY TO PICK when the tassels at the top of the cobs turn brown and the kernels release a milky liquid when pressed with a fingernail. Twist the cobs to remove them from the stem. ❶

Fruit in season

EARLY APPLES SUCH AS 'DISCOVERY' will be ready to pick at the end of the month. **2**

BLACKBERRIES RIPEN throughout August and early September. Pick the fruits daily and store in the refrigerator. Then eat, freeze or cook them within a couple of days.

LATE STRAWBERRIES and everbearers deliver a crop throughout August.

BLUEBERRIES COLOUR UP and are ready to harvest this month. Pick regularly to encourage more flowering and a longer cropping period. **3**

PLUM TREES ARE PRODUCING A HARVEST, their sweet fruits ready to pick if they feel soft when squeezed gently. Pick a few times this month and make jam or freeze any excess.

FEELING ADVENTUROUS? The pineapple guava (*Feijoa sellowiana*) is a large evergreen shrub that is best grown in pot of peat-free soil-based compost in the UK and given some winter protection in a greenhouse or cool conservatory over winter. If you can keep temperatures above 5°C (41°F), it may produce its large, beautiful red and pink flowers in summer, followed by green, egg-shaped fruits in the autumn. The sweet, aromatic fruits drop to the ground when ripe and taste of pineapple, apple and mint.

Recipe

PEA AND POTATO CURRY

Using the vegetables now ready for harvesting, including peas, potatoes, tomatoes and chillies, as well as herbs that you may also be growing the garden, this Asian-inspired recipe is an easy dish to rustle up for a summer evening meal. You can skip the chilli or halve the quantity if you prefer milder curries.

To puree the tomatoes, chop them into chunks, and heat gently (no water is needed) until they come to a boil, then simmer for 10 minutes. Leave to cool, and blitz in a blender for a few seconds.

1   Using a pestle and mortar, grind the coriander and cumin seeds. Heat the oil in large frying pan over a medium heat, add the potatoes and cook for 3–5 minutes, stirring occasionally. Transfer the potatoes to a bowl. Using the same pan, fry the crushed seeds and cook for about 30 seconds, then add the onion, garlic, ginger and chilli. Cook for a few minutes until translucent.

2   Mix in the spices and add the tomato puree. Cook for a further 3–4 minutes until thickened. Return the potatoes to the pan, add salt to taste, and add the water. Cover and cook for 15 minutes, checking after 10 minutes and adding more water if needed.

3   Add the peas and half the coriander and cook for a further 5 minutes. Serve with pilau or long grain rice and garnish with the remaining coriander.

INGREDIENTS

1 tsp coriander seeds
½ tsp cumin seeds
2 tbsp rapeseed oil
3 medium potatoes, cubed
I onion, finely chopped
4 cloves of garlic, finely chopped
2cm (1in) ginger, peeled and finely chopped
½ green chilli, finely chopped
½ tsp turmeric powder
½ tsp cayenne pepper
2 medium to large tomatoes, pureed
Pinch of salt
250ml (0.5pt) water
250g (8oz) peas
100g (3½oz) chopped fresh coriander

Challenges of the month

Potato blight (see p.145) may continue to be a problem and may also be found on tomatoes. Keeping plants healthy with the correct irrigation and drainage, particularly in dry conditions, will help to keep diseases at bay.

EARWIGS are omnivorous beetle-like insects, with a pair of pincers on their rear end, that feed on other small invertebrates and plants. However, while they may chew the petals of clematis, dahlias and chrysanthemums, they are also a useful pest predator, controlling aphid populations on fruit trees. With this in mind, you may wish to simply tolerate them in the garden, or trap them in upturned pots stuffed with straw and balanced on canes close to your flowers. The earwigs will take refuge in the pots and can be shaken out elsewhere in the garden, near fruit trees or where less susceptible plants are growing.

GLASSHOUSE RED SPIDER MITE is a sap-sucking insect that thrives in warm, dry conditions and causes mottled leaves and poor growth, or even plant death, in many species grown in greenhouses. The tiny, yellowish-green mites and white cast skins and egg shells can be seen on the undersides of leaves, but it is their fine webbing that is the most noticeable sign of their presence. Remove severely infested plants and minimize the number of overwintering mites by cleaning out debris in greenhouses in autumn. Biological controls are also available and highly effective against this mite.

CLEMATIS WILT is a fungal disease that affects large-flowered hybrid clematis cultivars, causing rapid wilting and, in severe cases, killing plants. The first signs are often spots on the leaves, which then shrivel and turn black, after which the stems wilt. To prevent it, plant the root ball about 5cm (2in) below the soil level and add a mulch to preserve moisture, which these plants prefer. If a clematis is infected, cut the wilted stems back to healthy growth and promptly destroy the affected material to prevent it contaminating the soil. New healthy shoots may then emerge from below the ground. Also disinfect pruning tools to prevent cross contamination to healthy plants. Wilting in other clematis is usually due to drought stress and they will probably revive after watering.

Look out for

The pipistrelle bat

The tiny pipistrelle bat (*Pipistrellus*) is native to the UK and the most common of our bat species. There are three types to look out for. The common pipistrelle (*Pipistrellus pipistrellus*) and soprano pipistrelle (*Pipistrellus pygmaeus*) are both widespread throughout the country and were thought to be one species until the 1990s when it was discovered that the frequency of their echolocation calls differed. The larger Nathusius' pipistrelle (*Pipistrellus nathusii*) is a rare species with small scattered populations found throughout the UK, from the Shetlands down to the Channel Islands. Both the common and soprano species have golden-brown fur, a slightly paler underside and a dark mask around the face, while the larger Nathusius' pipistrelle looks very similar but has longer fur on its upper body.

You may see pipistrelles darting about just after dusk in your garden or around street lamps, searching for midges, mosquitoes, moths and other night-flying insects, which they catch and eat on the wing. Despite their size – they weigh just 3–8g (0.1–0.3oz) – each bat can consume 3,000 insects in one night, helping to keep populations of biting insects and night-flying pests such as codling moth in check.

They roost in small colonies in tree holes, bat boxes and cavities in house roofs and walls, squeezing their little bodies into the tiniest of crevices. During the summer months, the females form larger maternity colonies and, after mating, each gives birth to a single pup, which they feed with their milk for three to four weeks. The young then take wing and are able to forage for themselves at six weeks old.

These little bats hibernate from November to April in smaller groups or singly, but may come out to feed on warm days.

Identifying dahlias

Loved for their showy blooms, dahlias come in a vast array of colours and shapes, and range in size from dwarf types just 30cm (12in) in height up to tall border plants of 1.5m (5ft) or more. These tuberous perennials are grouped by their flower shapes, and include the flat-faced single, peony and collerette dahlias, many of which attract bees; spiky-petalled cactus dahlias; spherical ball and pompon blooms; and the double-flowered decorative, anemone and waterlily-flowered cultivars. Most have green leaves, but some have dark burgundy or purple foliage. Plant the tubers in spring in sun and free-draining soil, then dig them up and bring them indoors after frost has blackened the foliage in autumn. In milder regions, you can leave the plants *in situ* with a thick mulch on top.

DAHLIA 'BISHOP OF LLANDAFF' AGM [PAEONY]
The semi-double, vibrant red flowers of this popular dahlia bloom from July to September above divided, dark bronze-red leaves.
H x S: 100 x 45cm (39 x 18in)

DAHLIA HAPPY SERIES AGM [SINGLE]
These popular dahlias produce a profusion of open single flowers that attract pollinators. They come in a range of colours, many with contrasting dark foliage.
H x S: up to 80 x 60cm (32 x 24in)

DAHLIA 'DAVID HOWARD' AGM [DECORATIVE]
This decorative dahlia produces a profusion of fully double, soft burnt-orange flowers against contrasting dark, bronze-tinged leaves.
H x S: 75 x 75cm (30 x 30in)

DAHLIA 'SMALL WORLD' AGM [POMPON]
Perfect for cutting, the miniature creamy-white pompon flowers of 'Small World' are held aloft on tall, sturdy stems over green foliage.
H x S: 100 x 45cm (39 x 18in)

DAHLIA 'CHAT NOIR' AGM [SEMI-CACTUS]
Tall stems of smouldering dark red spiky flowers, almost black in the centre, set off by bright green foliage, make an eye-catching statement in a bed or border.
H x S: 100 x 45cm (39 x 18in)

Garden tales

The opium poppy, *Papaver somniferum*, has been both gardener's friend and society's foe throughout history. The large, colourful flowers make it a garden favourite in the UK but the sap found in the seedpods is also used to make opiates and, for this reason, the plant's sale and cultivation are restricted in the US and other countries around the world. The seeds of this beautiful plant are also nutritious and non-toxic, and the opiates derived from

it are essential to the manufacture of important pharmaceutical drugs such as morphine, codeine and other pain relief medicines. However, its use in toxic and highly addictive narcotic drugs such as opium and heroin has devastating consequences for many people.

The ancient Greeks discovered that the poppy could be used as an analgesic, and its darker addictive side was acknowledged by Arabian physicians more than 900 years ago. However, despite its side-effects, opium was administered to wounded soldiers in the American Civil War and the First World War, many of whom went on to develop a dependence on it.

In 19th century China, the plant was the cause of the Opium Wars, fought by the British and French who wanted a legalized and free opium trade, and the Chinese government, which tried to ban its sale to save its citizens from addiction and premature death.

Today, morphine derived from the opium poppy continues to play an important role in relieving severe pain associated with cancer and other long-term illnesses, while we can also enjoy this elegant flower and its seedpods in the garden and the seeds in our cakes and bakes without harm.

Legend: Lily – the symbol of purity

A symbol of purity, devotion and fertility, the white lily (*Lilium*) has long been included in bridal flowers at weddings and has a special meaning in the Christian church. The lily is associated with the Annunciation to the Virgin Mary, and artists including Leonardo da Vinci and Botticelli depicted it being handed to Mary by the Angel Gabriel, while in other religious iconography the flower features in a vase standing between them.

The myth that may have given rise to the association between the flower and fertility can be traced back to Ancient Greece and the goddess Hera. Known as the Queen of the Gods, Hera was the wife of Zeus, who had an affair and a son, Hercules, with a mortal woman. Zeus tricked his wife into nursing the child, hoping her milk would endow him with special powers, by placing Hercules beside the Goddess's other children while she slept. When Hera awoke, she pulled the child from her breast and her milk spurted up to the heavens to create the Milky Way, while other drops fell to the ground and turned into lilies.

A similar myth relates to Hera's Roman counterpart Juno, the goddess who gave her name to the month of June. She is depicted in *The Origin of the Milky Way* by 16th century Italian painter Tintoretto with the milk spurting from her breast being transformed into stars.

The Easter lily (*Lilium longiflorum*) is also associated with rebirth and this sweetly scented species is believed to have grown where Christ's blood and tears fell during the crucifixion. It is also associated with the Resurrection in Christian iconography. However, this Asian species was unlikely to be known in biblical times and blooms in summer in the UK – it is cultivated here under glass for earlier flowers that coincide with Easter. The lily is also traditionally included at funerals to symbolize the soul in a renewed state of innocence when departing for heaven.

September

Soft light caresses the garden as summer bows out, imbuing it with jewelled hues and succulent fruits as the seasons turn. Trees and vegetable crops offer rich pickings this month, the surplus providing goodies to store and enjoy later during leaner times, while warm soil and showers make it a perfect time to sow and plant, in preparation for next year's bounty.

KEY EVENTS
RHS Wisley Flower Show, 3–8 September
International Day of Peace, 21 September
Autumn Equinox, 22 September
Michaelmas Day (*last day of the harvest season*), 29 September

What to do

Heralding the start of the autumn planting season for hardy perennials, bulbs and pot-grown shrubs, the warm soil and sunny days in late September provide ideal conditions for growth. It's also a good time to move any plants that have outgrown their allotted space or are in the wrong position. You can continue to sow small batches of lettuces and Oriental greens in the greenhouse or on a sunny windowsill for mini leaves later in the autumn and early winter. It is also wise to remove weeds and pick up diseased leaves and fallen stems from beds and borders.

In the garden

PLANT SPRING BULBS, such as daffodils, grape hyacinths (*Muscari*), crocuses and alliums. Wait until November to plant tulips, when colder temperatures may reduce the incidence of the fungal disease tulip fire. **1**

TAKE ROSE HARDWOOD CUTTINGS by removing a healthy shoot of pencil thickness and about 30cm (12in) long. Snip off the tip and all the leaves bar the uppermost three sets, and trim the base below a leaf joint. Make a slit trench by plunging a spade in the ground and plant the stems so that just the leaves are exposed.

PLANT OUT SPRING-FLOWERING BIENNIALS such as forget-me-nots (*Myosotis*) and wallflowers (*Erysimum*) that you sowed earlier in summer for a beautiful display next year.

SOW HARDY ANNUALS such as love-in-a-mist (*Nigella*), honesty (*Lunaria*) and poppies (*Papaver*) in a sheltered spot and free-draining soil for earlier blooms the following spring. **2**

PLANT SHRUBS, CLIMBERS AND PERENNIALS that have been grown in pots (bare-root plants are available later in autumn), checking that you have the right site and soil conditions for those you select.

SOW OR TURF LAWNS. September and October are the best months to establish a lawn, since grass seed germinates quickly now, and the roots of turf establish easily too. Remember not to walk over the area for a few weeks after sowing or laying a lawn. **3**

DIVIDE HARDY PERENNIALS, such as geraniums, crocosmia, phlox, sedums (*Hylotelephium*) and daylilies (*Hemerocallis*). See p.52 for details on how to divide them. **4**

In the fruit & veg patch

HARVEST AUTUMN RASPBERRIES AND BLACKBERRIES, freezing or making jam with any surpluses. **1**

PLANT ONION SETS in a sunny site at the beginning of the month, spacing the bulbs 8cm (3in) apart and burying them so that the pointed ends are just covered with soil. Apply an organic fertilizer now and again in spring to boost growth.

PLANT GARLIC BULBS in a sunny spot and free-draining soil. Space the cloves 15cm (6in) apart, with the tips 2.5cm (1in) below the soil surface.

PLANT NEW STRAWBERRY PLANTS at the beginning of the month so they can establish before winter sets in. Remember to keep them watered during dry spells. **2**

REMOVE TRUSSES OF UNRIPE TOMATOES at the end of the month. Bring them inside and place in a drawer or paper bag, together with a banana, which will release ethylene, a hormone that helps to speed up the ripening process.

Indoors

AS THE HOURS OF DAYLIGHT REDUCE, set sun-loving houseplants such as cacti and succulents that need some protection from strong rays in summer back into a brighter position.

STOP FEEDING YOUR INDOOR PLANTS now, as their growth slows down during autumn and may stop altogether over winter. Continue to water them regularly while temperatures are still warm.

BRING HOUSEPLANTS that have spent the summer outside back indoors, now that night-time temperatures are lower.

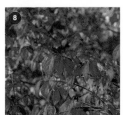

Plant now

1. Guelder rose (*Viburnum opulus*)
2. Bluebeard (*Caryopteris × clandonensis*)
3. Hardy ornamental grasses (such as *Calamagrostis varia*)
4. Rooper's red-hot poker (*Kniphofia rooperi*)
5. False sunflower (*Heliopsis helianthoides* var. *scabra*)
6. Bugbane (*Actaea simplex*)
7. Bistort (*Bistorta* species, syn. *Persicaria*)
8. Winged spindle (*Euonymus alatus* 'Compactus')
9. Pernettya (*Gaultheria mucronata*)
10. Firethorn (*Pyracantha* species and cultivars)
11. Geranium rose (*Rosa* 'Geranium')

Project: Cold-season basket

As summer starts to fade, plant up a hanging basket to offer colour from autumn through to the following spring, using a range of bulbs, small evergreen shrubs, leafy perennials and a few hardy flowers. Purchase the largest basket you can fit into your space and install a sturdy bracket for it in a bright position where you will be able to admire your display from inside your house.

Choose a selection of plants that will tolerate the cold months ahead. Good choices include small shrubs sold for winter container displays, heucheras, ferns such as the hart's tongue fern (*Asplenium scolopendrium*), common polypody (*Polypodium vulgare*) and soft shield fern (*Polystichum setiferum*), and flowering violas, primulas, polyanthus, forget-me-nots (*Myosotis*), and bellis daisies. While some of these blooms may flower intermittently through winter, in more exposed areas they will put on their best show from early spring. Also buy dwarf bulbs, such as narcissi, grape hyacinths (*Muscari*) and species tulips to add to the spring display.

To plant the basket, place it on a terracotta pot to stabilize it. Snip holes in baskets with integrated liners, or add a fabric liner, making sure it also has drainage holes in the base. Add about 5cm (2in) of peat-free multipurpose compost to the bottom of the basket and plant your bulbs, ensuring they are not touching each other. Then top up with more compost, to about 5cm (2in) from the rim. Add your plants, with the tallest in the centre and any trailing types flowing over the edges. The bulbs will push their way through the other plants in spring.

Water sparingly during prolonged dry periods in winter but apply more moisture in spring when the plants start to grow. Plants put on very little growth in winter and will not need any fertilizer until mid-spring.

Looking up

Sunrise and Sunset

The seasons are turning and days shortening as summer moves into autumn. Make the most of the waning sunlight to plant, sow and prune.

	LONDON		EDINBURGH	
	Sunrise	Sunset	Sunrise	Sunset
Sun, Sep 1	6:12:26 am	7:48:16 pm	6:16:32 am	8:08:39 pm
Mon, Sep 2	6:14:02 am	7:46:01 pm	6:18:29 am	8:06:03 pm
Tue, Sep 3	6:15:37 am	7:43:47 pm	6:20:26 am	8:03:27 pm
Wed, Sep 4	6:17:13 am	7:41:31 pm	6:22:23 am	8:00:50 pm
Thu, Sep 5	6:18:49 am	7:39:15 pm	6:24:20 am	7:58:13 pm
Fri, Sep 6	6:20:24 am	7:36:59 pm	6:26:17 am	7:55:35 pm
Sat, Sep 7	6:22:00 am	7:34:42 pm	6:28:13 am	7:52:57 pm
Sun, Sep 8	6:23:35 am	7:32:25 pm	6:30:10 am	7:50:19 pm
Mon, Sep 9	6:25:11 am	7:30:08 pm	6:32:07 am	7:47:41 pm
Tue, Sep 10	6:26:46 am	7:27:51 pm	6:34:03 am	7:45:02 pm
Wed, Sep 11	6:28:22 am	7:25:33 pm	6:36:00 am	7:42:23 pm
Thu, Sep 12	6:29:57 am	7:23:15 pm	6:37:56 am	7:39:44 pm
Fri, Sep 13	6:31:33 am	7:20:56 pm	6:39:53 am	7:37:05 pm
Sat, Sep 14	6:33:09 am	7:18:38 pm	6:41:50 am	7:34:26 pm
Sun, Sep 15	6:34:44 am	7:16:19 pm	6:43:46 am	7:31:46 pm
Mon, Sep 16	6:36:20 am	7:14:01 pm	6:45:43 am	7:29:07 pm
Tue, Sep 17	6:37:56 am	7:11:42 pm	6:47:40 am	7:26:27 pm
Wed, Sep 18	6:39:32 am	7:09:23 pm	6:49:36 am	7:23:48 pm
Thu, Sep 19	6:41:08 am	7:07:05 pm	6:51:33 am	7:21:08 pm
Fri, Sep 20	6:42:44 am	7:04:46 pm	6:53:30 am	7:18:29 pm
Sat, Sep 21	6:44:20 am	7:02:27 pm	6:55:27 am	7:15:49 pm
Sun, Sep 22	6:45:56 am	7:00:09 pm	6:57:24 am	7:13:10 pm
Mon, Sep 23	6:47:33 am	6:57:50 pm	6:59:21 am	7:10:30 pm
Tue, Sep 24	6:49:09 am	6:55:32 pm	7:01:19 am	7:07:51 pm
Wed, Sep 25	6:50:46 am	6:53:13 pm	7:03:16 am	7:05:12 pm
Thu, Sep 26	6:52:23 am	6:50:55 pm	7:05:14 am	7:02:33 pm
Fri, Sep 27	6:54:00 am	6:48:38 pm	7:07:12 am	6:59:55 pm
Sat, Sep 28	6:55:37 am	6:46:20 pm	7:09:10 am	6:57:16 pm
Sun, Sep 29	6:57:15 am	6:44:03 pm	7:11:08 am	6:54:38 pm
Mon, Sep 30	6:58:53 am	6:41:46 pm	7:13:07 am	6:52:01 pm

Moonrise and moonset

Moon Phases

● **NEW MOON** 3 September   ○ **FULL MOON** 18 September
◑ **FIRST QUARTER** 11 September   ◑ **THIRD QUARTER** 24 September

MONTH	LONDON			EDINBURGH		
	Moonrise	Moonset	Moonrise	Moonrise	Moonset	Moonrise
1	03:57	19:35		03:49	20:04	
2	05:12	19:48		05:11	20:10	
3	06:25	19:58		06:29	20:15	
4	07:35	20:07		07:45	20:19	
5	08:45	20:16		09:00	20:23	
6	09:54	20:26		10:16	20:28	
7	11:06	20:38		11:34	20:34	
8	12:19	20:53		12:54	20:43	
9	13:35	21:14		14:18	20:56	
10	14:50	21:44		15:41	21:18	
11	16:00	22:27		16:56	21:56	
12	16:58	23:29		17:54	22:58	
13	17:42			18:31		
14	-	00:47	18:13	-	00:24	18:53
15	-	02:15	18:35	-	02:02	19:06
16	-	03:48	18:52	-	03:44	19:16
17	-	05:21	19:06	-	05:25	19:23
18	-	06:53	19:19	-	07:05	19:29
19	-	08:25	19:32	-	08:44	19:36
20	-	09:58	19:47	-	10:25	19:44
21	-	11:32	20:07	-	12:07	19:56
22	-	13:03	20:34	-	13:48	20:14
23	-	14:27	21:13	-	15:20	20:45
24	-	15:37	22:06	-	16:33	21:36
25	-	16:28	23:13	-	17:20	22:47
26	-	17:03		-	17:48	
27	00:29	17:27		00:10	18:04	
28	01:46	17:44		01:35	18:15	
29	03:01	17:57		02:57	18:21	
30	04:14	18:07		04:17	18:26	

Average rainfall

The 20-year average rainfall for the UK in September is 116mm (4.6in), the same as for August, and temperatures may also match the summer months, so continue to water new and potted plants regularly this month.

LOCATION	DAYS	MM	INCHES
Aberdeen	10	61	2.4
Aberystwyth	13	97	3.8
Belfast	12	70	2.8
Birmingham	10	68	2.7
Bournemouth	9	69	2.7
Bristol	10	64	2.5
Cambridge	8	48	1.9
Canterbury	8	55	2.2
Cardiff	12	86	3.4
Edinburgh	10	55	2.2
Exeter	10	94	3.7
Glasgow	14	98	3.9
Gloucester	10	69	2.7
Inverness	12	63	2.5
Ipswich	8	49	1.9
Leeds	12	82	3.2
Liverpool	12	77	3.0
London	9	59	2.3
Manchester	13	98	3.9
Newcastle upon Tyne	9	45	1.8
Norwich	9	60	2.4
Nottingham	10	57	2.2
Oxford	9	62	2.4
Sheffield	9	63	2.5
Truro	12	77	3.0

Early-autumn abundance

Fruit and vegetable harvests peak in September and offer you the opportunity to share your produce with friends, and store, freeze or make jams and chutneys with any surpluses to enjoy later in winter.

As vegetable crops are cleared from the ground, consider using cover crops to salvage surplus nutrients, smother weeds and protect the soil from weather extremes over winter. These plants are unlikely to increase the incidence of diseases, and include cereals such as rye and oats (best sown before mid-September) and ryegrasses (suitable for later sowing into October). They also help to boost soil fertility when dug into the soil in spring.

FRUIT AND VEGETABLE HARVESTS
Most apples and pears that ripen in early September are best eaten fresh, while those that come later in the month and in October can be stored for winter use. All fruits should be harvested, even if they are diseased and thrown away; if left, they may harbour disease over winter. The same goes for any diseased shoots. However, you can place blemished fruits elsewhere in the garden to feed birds and other wildlife.

Potato and tomato blight often arrives in rainy weather in early autumn and can affect late tomato and potato crops. Once the foliage becomes infected, remove it, wait two weeks for the skins of the tubers to harden and then harvest them to eat fresh or store. Sadly, infected potatoes and tomatoes are not edible and must be disposed of, for example by burying them deeply.

SEEDS OF NEW LIFE
Rainy weather and ample soil nutrients, released by the decay of organic matter over summer, leads to a brief resurgence in growth in early autumn. However, by the end of the month, falling light levels begin to slow down growth again, which almost ceases in October. Sow seeds of hardy annual flowers and crops in early September to take advantage of this window of opportunity. Try annuals such as larkspurs and cornflowers, wild flowers, onion sets, overwintering lettuce and spinach.

September-sown lawns will also establish well and will be usable by spring. Existing lawns will have time to regrow and look good before winter, too, if spiked to aerate the soil (see p.101). Also rake out thatch, apply a low-nitrogen organic autumn fertilizer and sow seeds on bare patches.

PLANTS FOR FREE
Flower seeds can take months to ripen, so now is the time to collect them from early summer-flowering plants such as delphiniums and hardy geraniums. Also pot up or move self-sown seedlings of honesty and other spring-flowering plants. Cuttings of tender plants such as pelargoniums and fuchsias can be rooted now; overwinter in a bright frost-free place, such as a windowsill. Evergreen shrub cuttings taken using semi-ripe – neither soft nor woody – shoots can be placed in a cold frame to root. Those taken from *Choisya*, *Cistus*, *Berberis*, *Buxus* (box), hebes, lavender, mahonia, rosemary and thymes will have a good root ball by next May.

Edible garden

Continue to harvest ripe tomatoes growing under cover and outside, and aubergines, peppers and chillies in the greenhouse. The last of the sweetcorn, blackberries and blueberries will also be ripe for picking.

Veg in season

MARROWS AND COURGETTES provide a feast in early September, while winter squashes are continuing to develop, and may be ready to harvest by the end of the month. **1**

MAINCROP POTATOES continue to provide a harvest in September. Once the top growth has died down, lift the tubers, shake off the soil and leave them to dry before storing them in a hessian or strong paper bag in a cool, dry place. **2**

ROOT CROPS such as carrots, early parsnips and swedes that have attained a good size will be ready to pull up now. Both parsnips and swedes often taste sweeter after being frosted and can be left in the ground until then if not required sooner.

Fruit in season

APPLES AND PEARS ripen throughout September. To pick them, cup the fruit in the palm of your hand, then gently twist. Ripe fruits should come away from the tree easily. **3**

AUTUMN RASPBERRIES continue to provide a sweet treat in September. Eat fruits harvested on rainy days immediately, since the wet fruits will rot quickly. **4**

FIG TREES produce their sweet, dark-skinned fruits from early to mid-autumn. Ripe fruits produce a sticky sap at the base and are soft when squeezed.

FEELING ADVENTUROUS? Exotic-looking yellow or orange persimmons are easy to grow and the trees are surprisingly hardy, tolerating temperatures down to –10°C (14°F). Also known as kaki or sharon fruit (*Diospyros kaki*), they can grow up to 9m (30ft) over 20–30 years. Plant your tree in spring after the frosts in free-draining soil and full sun. The glossy dark green leaves turn bright yellow, orange and purple in the autumn, just as the tomato-shaped fruits ripen – they also store well for up to four months.

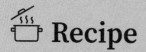 # Recipe

BLACKBERRY AND APPLE CRUMBLE

Make the most of your apple harvest and the last of the blackberries with this warm, comforting pudding. You can also make it later with fruits that were picked and frozen earlier in the summer, thawing them first. Cooking apples add some tartness to the flavour, but don't worry if you only have eaters – simply reduce the quantity of sugar so that the dish isn't too sweet. Conversely, add more sugar if you only have cooking apples to hand.

1   Heat the oven to 190°C (375°F/Gas 5). Place the plain flour and butter into a large bowl and rub together with your fingertips until it resembles fine breadcrumbs. Gently stir in the demerara sugar.

2   Peel and core the apples and slice them into a separate bowl, then add the blackberries and mix together. In a smaller bowl, combine the cornflour, cinnamon and sugar and then add them to the fruit, so the apples and blackberries are coated with the sugary mixture.

3   Spoon the fruit into the bottom of an ovenproof dish, pushing it down with the back of a spoon to form an even layer. Then top with the crumble. Bake for 45 minutes until the topping is golden brown and the fruit is bubbling hot. Leave to cool and serve with custard, ice cream or yoghurt.

INGREDIENTS
For the crumble topping
240g (8oz) plain flour
150g (5oz) butter, at room temperature, cut into small pieces
120g (4oz) demerara sugar

For the fruit base
2 large cooking apples and 3 eating apples (or 5 large apples of any variety)
250g (8½oz) blackberries
2–3 tsp cornflour
¼ tsp ground cinnamon
100–150g (3½–5oz) caster sugar to taste

To serve
Custard, ice cream or yoghurt

Challenges of the month

Warm, damp conditions in early autumn often give rise to fungal growths, and you may see toadstools popping up around the garden. The majority are harmless or even beneficial to the soil and plants, so do not worry unless plants alongside them are suffering. The most damaging fungi are often less obvious to the gardener.

PEAR RUST is a fungal disease that produces bright orange spots on the leaves of pear trees, as well as brown growths on lower leaf surfaces. In rare cases, it may cause lesions on the stems and branches. Pear rust also affects junipers, which develop swellings on their stems and jelly-like growths in spring. The fungus does not usually affect the fruit, and rarely causes much harm to the plants, so simply prune out affected areas.

ROOT ROTS are caused by the fungus-like *Phytophthora* species and often occur when plants are grown in waterlogged or poorly drained soil. In trees, it can cause wilting, yellow or brown foliage and branch dieback. These symptoms may also occur during periods of drought, so check the base of the stem or trunk for the characteristic red-brown rot with a cidery or sour smell. If this disease is to blame, remove infected plants and change the soil before replanting. Improving soil drainage can also reduce the risk of plants succumbing to this disease and other forms of rot in the future. Some plants are more susceptible than others; visit the RHS website (rhs.org.uk) for a list of resistant plants.

CODLING MOTH LARVAE are the cause of maggoty apples and pears. They tunnel into the fruit and feed on the core area – you may also see little holes where they have crawled out. This moth usually affects only a small number of fruit, so it's generally best to tolerate the damage, and encourage the pest's main predators such as beetles and birds into the garden (see p.25). Sticky pheromone traps hung in the tree to lure males and reduce the moth's reproduction rates will limit numbers further, but will not eliminate the problem entirely, while beneficial nematodes (biological controls) sprayed on the tree bark and soil beneath it in autumn may also reduce larvae numbers.

SCABS are caused by an airborne fungus, *Venturia inaequalis,* which produces olive-green velvety spots on the leaves of apple and pear trees. It may also cause cracks on twigs and brown or black scabby patches on the fruits. Minor attacks cause only slightly discoloured fruits, which are still edible, and should be tolerated. In more severe cases, prune out blistered or cracked twigs and in autumn remove fallen leaves and infected fruits, which harbour the fungus.

Look out for

The bumblebee

The most well-loved of our native bees, bumblebees (*Bombus* species) are easy to spot in the garden with their rounded bodies and furry coats. Buzzing from flower to flower in search of food, this valuable insect, together with other wild bees, is responsible for pollinating a host of edible crops and flowers. There are 24 species of bumblebee in the UK, including the garden, buff-tailed, red-tailed, white-tailed, heath and tree bumblebee, and they are found from the Shetlands in the north down to the southern tip of Cornwall. Bumblebees are not aggressive and sting only if threatened, but unlike honeybees they do not die afterwards.

The first bumblebees to emerge from hibernation in spring are the queens, which come out looking for food and a suitable nesting site. Flying in cooler conditions by vibrating and warming up their muscles, they nest in a range of places, from abandoned mouseholes to loft cavities and compost heaps. Their nests are made from dried grasses, topped with a ball of pollen mixed with a waxy substance, on which the queens lay about a dozen eggs that hatch into sterile female workers. These offspring then forage for pollen and nectar to feed subsequent batches of grubs, which include new queens and males later in the season. All the workers, males and old queens die off in late summer or autumn but in warmer areas, buff-tailed bumblebee queens may start a new colony and remain active throughout the year. The new queens of other species hibernate underground, storing sperm from the males to fertilize their eggs the following year.

Plant nectar- and pollen-rich flowers in your garden – look out for the RHS Plant for Pollinators label – and include a range that bloom throughout the year to provide a continuous food source for bumblebees. Also offer shallow dishes of water or a sloping-sided pond for the bees to drink from.

Identifying asters

This group of daisy-like flowers is celebrated for their pink, red, white, purple or blue blooms which appear from late summer to late autumn, illuminating the garden with their jewelled colours. Our parents and grandparents would have known these plants as asters or Michaelmas daisies, and they all used to be grouped under one genus. However, scientific analysis has revealed that they're actually five different species, so you may find your favourites now listed under the botanical names *Aster, Callistephus, Eurybia, Kalimeris,* or *Symphyotrichum*. All are easy to grow in a sunny spot with average garden soil, and most are perennial, blooming year after year, apart from the annual China aster (*Callistephus*).

MICHAELMAS DAISY
(*ASTER × FRIKARTII* 'MÖNCH')
A firm favourite, this pretty, disease-resistant aster bears longlasting lavender-blue flowers from late summer to mid-autumn.
H x S: 70 x 40cm (28 x 16in)

JAPANESE ASTER
(*KALIMERIS INCISA*)
Compact and resistant to mildew, the Japanese aster produces masses of small blue, white or pink flowers for a long period from June to September.
H x S: 90 x 60cm (36 x 24in)

WHITE WOOD ASTER (*EURYBIA DIVARICATA*)
In summer and autumn this woodland-edge plant produces clusters of small white starry flowers on dark stems over heart-shaped foliage.
H x S: 60 x 60cm (24 x24in)

CHINA ASTER
(*CALLISTEPHUS CHINENSIS*)
Easy to grow from seed in spring, this decorative annual produces a mass of large, single or double flowers in a broad spectrum of colours from late summer to autumn.
H x S: up to 70 x 40cm (28 x 16in)

NEW ENGLAND ASTER
(*SYMPHYOTRICHUM NOVAE-ANGLIAE*)
Many old favourites, including the former *Aster novae-belgii*, and this group with their clusters of colourful daisy flowers, have been reclassified as *Symphyotrichum*.
H x S: up to 1.5 x 1m (5 x 3ft)

Garden tales

History: The rise and fall of the apple orchard

As Britain provided the perfect climate and soil for growing apples, orchards used to be a common sight, offering a supply of fresh fruit to the local community each autumn. Sadly, over the past century we have lost half of all orchards in England and Wales and 80 per cent of traditionally managed orchards, along with many heritage fruit varieties.

Apple-growing has a long history in the UK, with the first orchards planted by Roman settlers. Expert apple-growers and cider-makers from Normandy then introduced new varieties in the Middle Ages when they arrived on our shores following the French invasion of 1066. An initiative to make the country more self-sufficient in the 16th and 17th centuries led to further expansion of fruit-growing areas, and by the 19th century many communities were blessed with a local apple orchard. Apples were grown on seedling rootstocks and were larger than modern trees, allowing wild flowers to grow beneath their spreading boughs. Beehives were also installed to ensure good pollination rates, a package that offered flowers in spring, honey in summer, fruit in autumn and a sanctuary for wildlife throughout the year.

By the mid 20th century, these small orchards were in decline, replaced by large commercial fruit farms that relied on pesticides to deliver uniform crops of just a few varieties. The rich biodiversity that thrived in traditional settings was lost and even commercial farms soon went into decline as cheap fruit imports from abroad flooded the market. Government subsidies to clear traditional orchards to make way for urban expansion, coupled with unprofitable large-scale farming, contributed to the demise of all commercial fruit production by the end of the century.

However, the table is turning once again as organizations such as the RHS and National Trust are planting new orchards and growing old heritage varieties once more, while encouraging greater biodiversity with eco-friendly management programmes.

Legend: Harvest celebrations

Harvest time has been imbued with special meaning throughout history. In Ancient Greece, people worshipped Demeter, the goddess of the harvest who presided over grains and the fertility of the earth, while in Rome they celebrated her counterpart, Ceres, the corn goddess.

In the UK, the whole community was responsible for bringing in the harvest, before the invention of the horse-drawn reaper-binder and, later, the combine harvester. Each man, woman and child had a role to play and their hard labour culminated in a Harvest Home supper laid on by the farmer as a thanks to the workers.

The last sheaf of corn was believed to hold the corn spirit and saved. Some communities would then leave the sheaf for birds to peck on New Year's Day, while others scattered it on the fields in spring, or wove the stems into corn dollies. The dollies were either burned and the ashes spread over the fields, or broken up and ploughed back into the soil as insurance for a good harvest the following year. While most resembled a man or woman, in some areas, the corn was woven into the shape of a bell, chandelier or crown.

Another local tradition of farming communities in Devon and Cornwall was 'Crying the Neck', where the harvesters would call to one another, culminating in the 'neck' or last sheaf of corn being bound with ribbon and kept, ensuring a good harvest in the year to come.

Prior to Henry VIII splitting from the Catholic Church, the religious festival of Michaelmas, or the Feast of Michael and All Angels, was celebrated on the 29th September to mark the end of the harvest. At this festival commemorating Archangel Michael, who defeated Satan in the war of heaven, a roast goose fattened on the stubble of the harvest field was served to mark the occasion. The traditional Harvest Festival, celebrated in church, came later. It is thought to have been started in the 1800s by Cornish vicar Reverend Robert Hawker, who gathered his parishioners to sing hymns of thanks, such as 'We plough the fields and scatter' and 'All things bright and beautiful'.

> Each man, woman and child had a role to play and their hard labour culminated in a Harvest Home supper laid on by the farmer as a thanks to the workers.

October

As the nights draw in and temperatures fall, October offers one final gift to share before winter, when the garden fires up for a spectacular swansong. Glistening fruits deliver their sweet feast while trees and shrubs that have gone unnoticed all year now dance in the spotlight, their crimson, orange and gold leaves falling like coins around a treasure chest.

KEY EVENTS

RHS Taste of Autumn Food Festival (at RHS Garden Hyde Hall),
  4–6 October
Yom Kippur, 12 October
Apple Day (*celebration of British apples*), 21 October
British Summer Time ends, 27 October
Halloween, 31 October

What to do

Planting pot-grown hardy shrubs, climbers and perennials continues as we approach mid-autumn. Choose a frost-free, dry day for planting and make sure the soil is not too wet – digging damp soil can lead to compaction and poor growth. You can also continue to plant spring bulbs for next year's flowers and harvest apples and pears that are ripe for picking. Plant garlic and shallot sets, if you didn't have time last month (see p.174), and pick and freeze herbs for use over winter.

In the garden

RAKE OR SCARIFY THATCH (DEAD GRASS AND MOSS) and debris from between the grass blades in a lawn and add it to the compost heap. To improve drainage and the health of the grass, aerate the soil by pushing a fork into the ground at 15cm (6in) intervals across the lawn, then fill them with a lawn top dressing, brushing over the surface with a stiff broom. **1**

REMOVE FALLEN LEAVES from the surface of small ponds with a rake to prevent them sinking to the bottom and decomposing. The additional nutrients they then release into the water can build up in small water features and feed algae and other pond weeds. Also remove pumps for the winter. **2**

RAKE LEAVES from lawns, patios and pathways. You can then use them to make leafmould by packing them into old compost bags with a few holes pierced in the base, or storing them in a structure made from wire mesh. The decomposed leaves can be used as a mulch after about a year. **3**

LIFT AND STORE TENDER BULBS, such as gladioli and begonias. Remove the excess soil clinging to them and leave them to dry off before storing in a cool, dry, frost-free place over winter. They can then be replanted the following year. Ensure there is good air circulation to prevent them rotting. Dahlias can be left in situ in milder areas of the country with a thick mulch placed over the roots.

In the fruit & veg patch

MULCH BEDS WITH HOMEMADE COMPOST, laying a 5cm (2in) layer over the soil surface between your crops.

PRUNE BLACKBERRIES after they have fruited. Remove all the stems that fruited this year, leaving the new growth that emerged during the spring and summer. Tie the new stems on to their supports.

LIFT POTATOES, CARROTS AND BEETROOTS on a dry day. Ensure all crops are disease-free and dry before storing them in a cool, dry, frost-free area. Place potatoes in paper or hessian sacks; store carrots and beetroot in boxes, in layers of used compost. ❶

FOR AN EARLY SUMMER CROP, sow broad beans outside in trenches 5cm (2in) deep, from late October into early November. Cover with soil and fleece or a cloche to prevent mice digging them up. Good varieties for autumn sowing include 'Aquadulce Claudia' or 'The Sutton'. ❷

Indoors

CHECK PLANTS FOR BUGS and wash or pick them off as soon as you see them to prevent an infestation.

FORCE HYACINTH BULBS for a midwinter indoor display. In early October, plant 'prepared' or 'heat-treated' bulbs in a bowl with drainage holes in the base, setting them close together but not touching on a 5cm (2in) layer of compost. Top up the bowl with more compost, leaving the pointed tips of the bulbs visible. Water lightly and cover them. Keep the bulbs in a dark, cool, frost-free area for about ten weeks until shoots appear, then move to a light, airy spot indoors to flower.

Plant now

1 Smoke bush (*Cotinus* species and cultivars)
2 Spring-flowering bulbs (such as *Crocus* 'Flower Record')
3 Winter pansies (*Viola* species)
4 Pot-grown trees (such as fig trees)
5 Virginia creeper (*Parthenocissus* species)
6 Late-season clematis (such as *C.* 'Bill MacKenzie')
7 Heavenly bamboo (*Nandina domestica*)
8 Beauty berry (*Callicarpa bodinieri* var. *giraldii* 'Profusion')
9 Oleaster (*Elaeagnus* species)
10 Enkianthus (*Enkianthus campanulatus*)
11 Spindle tree (*Euonymus europaeus* 'Red Cascade')

Project: Fernery

Loved by the Victorians, ferneries were the height of fashion during the 19th century when collections of these leafy shade-lovers were a must-have for rich and poor alike. Ferns' lacy fronds still have wide appeal, their colours and textures brightening up gloomy areas of the garden where many plants would struggle to thrive.

To make a fernery in your garden, dig out a bed in a partly shaded spot at the edge of a tree canopy or beside a garden wall or fence. Then choose a selection of ferns of different heights and shapes, combining evergreens with deciduous types, which will turn a bronze colour overwinter, and making sure that they suit your soil conditions. Many ferns like moist soil, so if yours is free-draining, opt for male ferns (*Dryopteris*), the soft shield fern (*Polystichum setiferum*), diminutive polypodies (*Polypodium vulgare*) and the hart's tongue fern (*Asplenium scolopendrium*), with its wavy-edged shiny evergreen leaves. If you want to inject a colour contrast, try the silvery Japanese painted fern (*Athyrium niponicum*) or *Dryopteris erythrosora* 'Brilliance', with its orangy-red young foliage; both tolerate dry soils.

Place the tallest ferns at the back and smaller plants at the front, combining a few of each variety, if you have

space. You can also include old tree stumps or logs to create a naturalistic woodland-floor effect, and some spring bulbs to provide colour in between the deciduous ferns before their new fronds unfurl later in the season.

Water regularly in dry weather until the plants are established and they will then largely look after themselves. Just cut away the old growth of deciduous plants in spring to make way for the new fronds that will elegantly unfurl as the season progresses.

Looking up

Sunrise and Sunset

The shorter days offer little time for busy gardeners at this time of year, when the temperatures are still high enough for new plants to establish before winter sets in.

	LONDON		EDINBURGH	
	Sunrise	Sunset	Sunrise	Sunset
Tue, Oct 1	7:00:30 am	6:39:29 pm	7:15:05 am	6:49:23 pm
Wed, Oct 2	7:02:09 am	6:37:13 pm	7:17:04 am	6:46:46 pm
Thu, Oct 3	7:03:47 am	6:34:57 pm	7:19:04 am	6:44:09 pm
Fri, Oct 4	7:05:26 am	6:32:42 pm	7:21:03 am	6:41:33 pm
Sat, Oct 5	7:07:05 am	6:30:27 pm	7:23:03 am	6:38:57 pm
Sun, Oct 6	7:08:44 am	6:28:13 pm	7:25:03 am	6:36:22 pm
Mon, Oct 7	7:10:23 am	6:25:59 pm	7:27:03 am	6:33:47 pm
Tue, Oct 8	7:12:03 am	6:23:45 pm	7:29:04 am	6:31:13 pm
Wed, Oct 9	7:13:43 am	6:21:33 pm	7:31:05 am	6:28:39 pm
Thu, Oct 10	7:15:23 am	6:19:21 pm	7:33:06 am	6:26:06 pm
Fri, Oct 11	7:17:04 am	6:17:09 pm	7:35:08 am	6:23:34 pm
Sat, Oct 12	7:18:44 am	6:14:59 pm	7:37:10 am	6:21:02 pm
Sun, Oct 13	7:20:26 am	6:12:49 pm	7:39:12 am	6:18:31 pm
Mon, Oct 14	7:22:07 am	6:10:40 pm	7:41:14 am	6:16:01 pm
Tue, Oct 15	7:23:49 am	6:08:31 pm	7:43:17 am	6:13:32 pm
Wed, Oct 16	7:25:31 am	6:06:24 pm	7:45:20 am	6:11:03 pm
Thu, Oct 17	7:27:13 am	6:04:17 pm	7:47:24 am	6:08:35 pm
Fri, Oct 18	7:28:56 am	6:02:11 pm	7:49:28 am	6:06:08 pm
Sat, Oct 19	7:30:39 am	6:00:07 pm	7:51:32 am	6:03:43 pm
Sun, Oct 20	7:32:22 am	5:58:03 pm	7:53:36 am	6:01:18 pm
Mon, Oct 21	7:34:05 am	5:56:00 pm	7:55:41 am	5:58:54 pm
Tue, Oct 22	7:35:49 am	5:53:59 pm	7:57:46 am	5:56:31 pm
Wed, Oct 23	7:37:33 am	5:51:58 pm	7:59:51 am	5:54:09 pm
Thu, Oct 24	7:39:17 am	5:49:59 pm	8:01:57 am	5:51:48 pm
Fri, Oct 25	7:41:01 am	5:48:01 pm	8:04:02 am	5:49:29 pm
Sat, Oct 26	7:42:46 am	5:46:04 pm	8:06:08 am	5:47:11 pm
Sun, Oct 27	6:44:31 am	4:44:09 pm	7:08:15 am	4:44:54 pm
Mon, Oct 28	6:46:16 am	4:42:15 pm	7:10:21 am	4:42:38 pm
Tue, Oct 29	6:48:01 am	4:40:22 pm	7:12:27 am	4:40:24 pm
Wed, Oct 30	6:49:46 am	4:38:31 pm	7:14:34 am	4:38:12 pm
Thu, Oct 31	6:51:31 am	4:36:41 pm	7:16:41 am	4:36:00 pm

Moonrise and moonset

Moon Phases

● **NEW MOON** 2 October   ○ **FULL MOON** 17 October
◑ **FIRST QUARTER** 10 October   ◑ **THIRD QUARTER** 24 October

MONTH	LONDON			EDINBURGH		
	Moonrise	Moonset	Moonrise	Moonrise	Moonset	Moonrise
1	05:25	18:17		05:33	18:31	
2	06:34	18:26		06:48	18:35	
3	07:44	18:36		08:04	18:39	
4	08:55	18:47		09:20	18:44	
5	10:08	19:00		10:40	18:52	
6	11:23	19:19		12:03	19:03	
7	12:38	19:45		13:26	19:21	
8	13:49	20:22		14:44	19:53	
9	14:51	21:16		15:48	20:44	
10	15:38	22:25		16:31	21:59	
11	16:13	23:47		16:57	23:30	
12	16:37			17:13		
13	-	01:16	16:55	-	01:07	17:23
14	-	02:46	17:10	-	02:45	17:31
15	-	04:16	17:23	-	04:23	17:37
16	-	05:47	17:36	-	06:02	17:44
17	-	07:20	17:51	-	07:42	17:51
18	-	08:55	18:08	-	09:25	18:01
19	-	10:30	18:32	-	11:10	18:16
20	-	12:02	19:06	-	12:51	18:42
21	-	13:21	19:55	-	14:17	19:25
22	-	14:22	20:59	-	15:16	20:31
23	-	15:03	22:14	-	15:52	21:52
24	-	15:32	23:32	-	16:12	23:19
25	-	15:51		-	16:24	
26	00:49	16:05		00:43	16:32	
27	01:03	15:16		01:04	15:37	
28	02:14	15:26		02:21	15:42	
29	03:24	15:35		03:36	15:46	
30	04:33	15:45		04:51	15:50	
31	05:44	15:55		06:07	15:55	

Average rainfall

October is the second wettest month of the year in the UK, with a 20-year average rainfall of 159mm (6.3in). This provides natural irrigation for newly planted hardy shrubs, climbers and perennials.

LOCATION	DAYS	MM	INCHES
Aberdeen	14	100	3.9
Aberystwyth	16	123	4.8
Belfast	14	96	3.8
Birmingham	12	81	3.2
Bournemouth	13	101	4.0
Bristol	13	86	3.4
Cambridge	10	59	2.3
Canterbury	11	80	3.1
Cardiff	15	129	5.0
Edinburgh	12	76	3.0
Exeter	15	159	6.3
Glasgow	16	132	5.2
Gloucester	13	80	3.1
Inverness	14	78	3.0
Ipswich	10	60	2.4
Leeds	14	98	3.9
Liverpool	14	90	3.5
London	11	79	3.1
Manchester	15	117	4.6
Newcastle upon Tyne	11	55	2.2
Norwich	11	70	2.8
Nottingham	11	72	2.8
Oxford	11	73	2.9
Sheffield	13	79	3.1
Truro	15	108	4.3

Composting autumn's bounty

Spent plants and other waste from the garden are full of plant nutrients that can be saved for next year by composting them. Stems, leaves and flowers will ultimately rot down if gathered together in a big heap on the ground and left to their own devices, but for uniform results delivered in less time, try a more systematic approach. The most efficient method is to fill a compost bin, at least one cubic metre in capacity, with garden and kitchen green waste. Aim for 20–50 per cent soft green materials (vegetable peelings and lawn mowings) and the remainder woody or straw-like plant matter such as dried flower stems, leaves and ripped up cardboard.

BIG IS BEST

If you have a smaller bin or are filling a larger one more slowly, it will not generate the heat needed for fast composting, but it will still rot down over time. However, in autumn, masses of materials are available and quickly filling a large bin may be possible. The decomposers in the bin will then create sufficient heat to speed up the composting process. If you have space, include two or more compost bins, so you can continue to add to one when the other is filled.

The high temperatures produced by the rotting mass in a large bin not only accelerate the composting process but also kill disease spores and weeds. Once the initial heat subsides the bin can be emptied, the contents mixed and the bin refilled, a process called 'turning'. A 'second heat' then follows and you should have sweet-smelling, usable compost in just a few months. Some gardeners capture the heat by building their compost bins against their greenhouse wall or within the greenhouse to save on fuel costs.

If the contents of the bin are mouldy, it is too dry and you should add some water. Slimy material is too wet and may lead to anaerobic conditions, the by-product of which is methane, a potent greenhouse gas. To remedy this, empty the bin and mix in woody material and pieces of cardboard before refilling the bin, then cover it to protect it from rain.

HOT BOX BINS

You will still create good compost if you fill your bin over time, but it will not generate the heat needed to kill as many unwanted organisms and the process will take longer. However, highly insulated 'hot box' bins generate heat even if filled in stages, as long as you include the right mix of materials. You also do not need to turn the contents of a hot box. Although more expensive than simple bins, they are smart, space-saving and rodents are less able get in.

To deter rodents in a more open bin, avoid cooked food or meat and use steel mesh to reinforce the floor and sides. A close-fitting lid will also exclude them.

WORMERIES

Wormeries consist of a box into which you add garden waste and unwanted food, except meat, fish and greasy products. Brandling worms 'work' this material into organic matter and also produce a liquid fertilizer, which is collected in a lower container. After a few months, when the compost is ready, it can be applied to the garden, after salvaging the worms for reuse.

Next month tree and shrub leaves will fall. Collect these in a wire cage or old compost bags to make leaf mould, a brown crumbly material with excellent soil-improving properties that can also be used in potting composts (see p.41).

Edible garden

Most root crops are best harvested now before the autumn rains increase soil moisture levels, which may cause them to rot. However, you can leave them in the ground for longer if you have sandy soil conditions.

Veg in season

ROOT CROPS such as potatoes, carrots and beetroots can be harvested now and stored for winter use (see p.194). Parsnips taste sweeter if left in the ground until they have been frosted.

CABBAGES SOWN IN SPRING are ready to harvest in October, providing vitamin-rich leaves to sustain you through the autumn.

STORED ONIONS AND GARLIC provide ingredients for autumn and winter dishes (see p.224). **1**

WINTER SQUASHES such as pumpkins should be harvested now before the first frosts. Leave a longish stalk on them and allow them to dry in the sun before storing. **2**

Fruit in season

MID- AND LATE-SEASON APPLES AND PEARS will be ready to pick in October (see p.182). Store in slatted crates that offer good ventilation, arranging the fruits in a single layer, and place in a cool, frost-free place. Check fruits regularly for signs of rot, and bring pears into the warmth to soften when they change colour but are still hard. Ideally, store mid- and late-season fruits separately.

THE LAST OF THE AUTUMN RASPBERRIES will also be ripe now.

FEELING ADVENTUROUS? The medlar (*Mespilus germanica*) is not widely grown in UK gardens, but should be more popular since it's very easy to care for. This small tree or large shrub produces little apple-shaped brown fruits in October and November that are hard and bitter until after they have been picked and stored indoors, a process known as 'bletting', when they soften and develop their unique sweet flavour. The trees are self-fertile, so you need only one to produce a crop. Plant your medlar in a warm, sunny location on free-draining soil. **3**

# Recipe

PUMPKIN PIE

This traditional American dish offers a sweet treat that makes the most of pumpkins grown in the garden that mature this month. Alternatively, you can buy them if your plot is not big enough for the rambling plants. Harvest your pumpkins before the frosts and leave them to dry in a warm, sunny spot – bring them inside if rain or frost is forecast. Once 'cured' in this way, they will store for up to six months in a cool, frost-free, well-ventilated place no colder than 10°C (50°F).

1   Heat the oven to 220°C (420°F/Gas 7). To make the pastry, using your fingertips, rub the butter into the flour until it resembles fine breadcrumbs. Mix in the icing sugar and add about 6–7 tablespoons of water to make a stiff dough.

2   Roll out the pastry until it is large enough to line a loose-bottomed 23cm/9in tart tin, pinching the edges when in place. Chill in the refrigerator for 15 minutes, then place baking parchment over the pastry and pour baking beans on top. Bake blind for 8 minutes. Remove the parchment and beans and return to the oven for 2–3 minutes.

3   Reduce the oven temperature to 150°C (300°F/Gas 3). To cook the pumpkin, place the cubes in a large pan, cover with water and bring to the boil, then simmer for 15 minutes or until tender. Drain and allow the pumpkin to cool.

4   Mash the pumpkin with a fork or puree it in a blender, then mix it in a bowl with the remaining ingredients. Pour into the pastry case and bake in the oven for about 30–40 minutes until the filling is set. Remove and leave to cool, then serve with whipped cream or ice cream.

INGREDIENTS
For the pastry
125g (4oz) cold butter
200g (7oz) plain flour
2 tbsp icing sugar

For the filling
450g (16oz) cubed
   pumpkin
180g (6oz) caster
   sugar
1 tsp ground cinnamon
1 tsp ground nutmeg
½ tsp ground ginger
½ tsp mixed spice
3 eggs, beaten

To serve
Whipped cream or ice
   cream

Challenges of the month

Fungal diseases continue to be the main cause for concern in October, many of the most harmful affecting trees and shrubs. Be vigilant and check your plants regularly for signs of disease, so that you can remove affected growth promptly before it spreads.

HONEY FUNGUS is a serious fungal infection that can kill trees and shrubs. Honey-coloured toadstools appear at the base of plants in late September and early October, but check for other symptoms, too, before diagnosing honey fungus, since many other fungi growing close to trees are harmless. Signs include a white fungal growth close to the ground between the bark and the wood, and black shoelace-like structures, known as rhizomorphs, below the soil surface near the base of the plant, which do not look like regular tree roots. There is no cure for honey fungus and affected trees will have to be removed to prevent it spreading to other woody plants. You can also install a vertical barrier to stop the rhizomorphs from spreading: surround the infected plant with heavy-duty plastic sheets 45cm (18in) deep in the soil, with 2–3cm (1in) above the surface.

SILVER LEAF is a fungal disease that causes the foliage of *Malus* and *Prunus* tree species, including apples, cherries and plums, to turn a silvery colour, hence the name. Fungal growths that have whitish woolly upper surfaces and are purple-brown below also occur from late summer, and cut stems have irregular dark stains on the inner wood.

To prevent silver leaf, prune susceptible plants in summer when there are fewer fungal spores around and wounds heal more quickly. If infection takes hold, remove the diseased stems before the fungal growths appear, cutting off the branch 10–15cm (4–6in) beyond the area of infection to wood that shows no sign of the dark staining. Sterilize the blades of cutting tools between each cut to prevent reinfection. Burn the diseased stems or put them in the household waste.

CORAL SPOT is a fungal disease that can affect many trees and woody plants, and may result in stem die-back in severe cases. The disease often infects trees grown in poor or unsuitable conditions or it can attack plants that have been pruned badly. Symptoms include small coral-pink raised spots on branches after they have died. To prevent the disease, ensure your tree is growing in the conditions it enjoys. Also, prune trees during dry weather (the fungal spores spread quickly during wet weather) and cut branches through the slight swelling at the base, known as the 'collar', rather than flush with the trunk or main stem. Remove all dead and diseased wood, cutting it back to healthy growth.

Look out for

The waxwing

One of the most beautiful avian migrants to the UK in winter is the waxwing (*Bombycilla garrulus*). These colourful birds fly here from their native Scandinavia, with visiting populations varying from year to year, depending on the availability of food. In mild years, only a few will arrive on our shores, but when food is scarce in their homelands, large flocks may appear, in an event known as an 'irruption'.

The first arrivals to Britain each winter can be seen along the east coast, from Scotland to East Anglia, but the birds often then move inland in search of their favourite berries, such as rowan, sorbus and hawthorn, although you may also see them feeding on cotoneaster fruit and rose hips. This starling-sized bird is easy to identify, with a light brown body, black throat and black mask around the eyes, set off by a distinctive tuft of orangy-red and pale peachy-brown feathers on its head. The wings are decorated with black, white, yellow and red markings, and the tail has a yellow tip. Waxwings are named after the bright red marks on some of their wing feathers, which look like drops of sealing wax. You may also be alerted to a flock of waxwings by their tinkling bell-like call before you see them.

The birds breed in coniferous forests, often near water, making a cup-shaped nest in a tree or bush in which the female lays a clutch of 3–7 eggs. The hatchlings emerge about two weeks later and fledge after 14–16 days. The good news regarding the waxwing is that healthy population numbers and extensive breeding grounds mean that it is classified as being of least concern by the International Union for Conservation of Nature.

Identifying *Hylotelephium* (syn. *Sedum)*

Formerly known as *Sedum* but now classified as *Hylotelephium*, these late-flowering perennials produce flat or domed heads of tiny pink or white blooms that glow in the autumn sun and attract a host of pollinators to the garden. The seedheads also offer a sanctuary for overwintering insects, which in turn provide food for birds. There are just a few species from which many cultivars have been bred, the most popular being *H. spectabile* and *H. telephium*, and the smaller, spreading *H. ewersii* and *H. sieboldii*. Grow these beauties in full sun or part shade and well-drained soil. If the taller species are prone to sprawling, give them the 'Chelsea chop' by cutting the stems back by half in late May (see p.93).

STONECROP (*HYLOTELEPHIUM TELEPHIUM* (ATROPURPUREUM GROUP) 'PURPLE EMPEROR' AGM)
The dark, purple-bronze fleshy leaves and dark red stems provide a foil for clusters of small, pale purplish-pink flowers from late summer to October.
H x S: 45 x 45cm (18 x 18in)

ROSE CARPET (*HYLOTELEPHIUM EWERSII* VAR. *HOMOPHYLLUM* 'ROSENTEPPICH')
This low-growing, spreading alpine species with blue-green leaves and large heads of tiny raspberry-pink, star-shaped flowers prefers a position in full sun.
H x S: 10 x 30cm (4 x 12in)

OCTOBER DAPHNE (*HYLOTELEPHIUM SIEBOLDII* 'MEDIOVARIEGATUM' AGM)
Spreading red stems carry bright green and cream variegated leaves, often edged in pink, while flat heads of rose-pink star-shaped flowers appear from late summer.
H x S: 20 x 45cm (8 x 18in)

STONECROP (*HYLOTELEPHIUM* 'LIME ZINGER' (PBR) (SUNSPARKLER SERIES))
The ground-hugging 'Lime Zinger' has pink-edged apple green leaves that offer ornamental value even before the starry pink flowers appear in late summer and autumn.
H x S: 20 x 45cm (8 x 18in)

ICE PLANT (*HYLOTELEPHIUM* (HERBSTFREUDE GROUP) 'HERBSTFREUDE' AGM)
Also known as *Sedum* 'Autumn Joy', this sun-lover combines bright green leaves and flat heads of salmon-pink flowers that mature to coppery-red in early autumn.
H x S: 60 x 60cm (24 x 24in)

Garden tales

History: Yew – a grave matter

Walk into any historic churchyard in Britain and you will almost certainly come across a yew (*Taxus baccata*) shading the gravestones. In fact, the tree's association with death and resurrection predates Christianity, and it was held sacred by the ancient Celts, who recognized its longevity and the ease with which it regenerates – as the central trunk ages, it sends up new shoots that can form large clumps, often with a hollow centre where the oldest wood has died out. The tree is also poisonous, and its leaves in particular are highly toxic, which explains why it was viewed by many cultures as an omen of death.

As Christianity became the dominant religion in Britain, these associations with yew trees continued, and branches were carried at funerals and waved on Palm Sunday, seven days before Easter. It is also believed that yews were planted over the graves of plague victims to protect and purify the dead, although their appearance in churchyards may simply be because they were removed from agricultural fields, where they would poison grazing animals, and left to grow only in these protected environments.

While many trees are established in or beside graveyards, evidence shows that others were growing in these areas long before the churches were built. The ancient yew beside Fortingall's church in Scotland, for example, is estimated to be many thousand years old, and legend has it that the Roman Emperor Pontius Pilate was born under it or climbed the branches as a child.

Yew's hard, close-grained wood was used to make medieval English longbows and crossbows. Today, it's used for gates, furniture, parquet flooring and wall panelling, and the compounds in its leaves and bark, known as 'taxanes', are in some anti-cancer drugs. The branches and red berries also provide nesting sites and winter sustenance for many birds, although the seeds are highly poisonous to humans.

Legend: The very British traditions of Halloween

You may think that dressing up at Halloween, trick or treating and carving pumpkins into ghoulish effigies are all commercial ideas brought here from America but, in fact, all these traditions have their roots in Britain.

Some Halloween customs date back to the festival of Samhain, which was celebrated by the ancient Celts on 31 October to mark the beginning of winter, when it was believed that the dead returned to Earth. Bonfires were lit and sacrifices made to honour the dead, and people disguised themselves in animal skins to drive away phantoms. The Christians continued some of these traditions, but with a slightly different emphasis. The 31st October was known as 'All Hallows' Eve', as it was one day before All Saints' Day, a celebration of 'hallowed' or 'holy' people, but the day when people remembered the dead took place a day after that on 2 November, which was All Souls' Day.

Carving pumpkins and the tradition of 'trick or treating' were also first established in Britain. Turnips were harvested in autumn, hollowed out and carved to resemble demons on All Souls' Day. Known as 'punkies' or 'Jack o' Lanterns', they represented the spirits of the dead who were thought to roam the marshes, and candles were placed inside to make them glow in the dark.

The poor also visited wealthier homes at this time, where they would be given 'soul cakes' in exchange for prayers for the owners' dead relatives, a custom known as 'souling'. In Scotland and Ireland, young people dressed up in costumes, sang a song, recited poetry or told jokes in exchange for fruit, nuts or money, rather than praying for the dead, and in some parts of the UK, Halloween was known as 'Mischief Night', when naughty children would knock on doors, make ghostly noises and run away to scare their neighbours.

As people emigrated from Britain to America, they took these traditions with them. Pumpkins, which were in plentiful supply there and easy to carve, were substituted for the hard turnips used in their homelands. The more commercialized trick or treating tradition was reintroduced in the 1950s when wartime sugar rationing was lifted. Candy companies eager to sell their wares launched advertising campaigns to encourage dressing up and giving their products to children.

The poor would be given 'soul cakes' in exchange for prayers for the owners' dead relatives.

November

The return of cold weather in late autumn marks the end of the growing year, yet there's still much to enjoy in the dying embers of the November garden. Spiders' webs touched by frost glitter like crystal chandeliers in the early-morning sun, and fiery foliage blazes bright against bleached stems, while carpets of crisp leaves crunch underfoot.

KEY EVENTS
Diwali/Deepavali, 1 November
Guy Fawkes Day, 5 November
Remembrance Sunday, 10 November
St Andrew's Day, 30 November

What to do

While the work in the garden slows down in late autumn, it is one of the best times to plant trees and shrubs. Bulbs are also still available and will flower reliably in spring when planted in November – you may find them at reduced prices, too. In the vegetable patch, you can plant garlic (see p.174) if you haven't already done so and the soil is not frozen or waterlogged. Also mulch your beds with well-rotted compost.

In the garden

PLANT TULIP BULBS, which may be at less risk of developing tulip fire fungal disease at this time of year. **1**

MOVE TERRACOTTA AND CLAY POTS that are vulnerable to cracking in cold temperatures before the frosts arrive. Bring those containing dormant plants into a shed and evergreen potted plants into a greenhouse or place close to a protective house wall. **2**

PLANT BARE-ROOT TREES AND SHRUBS, which are available from November to March. Make sure you plant them at the same depth as they were growing in their nursery beds, indicated by a darker soil mark on their stems (see p.216 on planting trees). **3**

PLANT ROSES, which are also available as bare-root plants now. Mix some organic matter such as home-made compost or well-rotted manure into the planting area. Mycorrhizal fungi root powder sprinkled on the roots on planting also works well; this is usually available when you buy the roses from the nursery. To plant, dig a hole twice as wide as the root ball and a little deeper. Make sure the knobbly graft union on the lower main stem is at soil level after planting, or follow the planting instructions that come with the rose.

PLANT OUT SPRING BEDDING such as primulas, wallflowers (*Erysimum*), and forget-me-nots (*Myosotis*).

ORDER SEEDS CATALOGUES – browsing online is another option but some companies also produce beautiful printed catalogues to inspire you.

In the fruit & veg patch

PLANT BARE-ROOT FRUIT TREES and bushes, planting them at the same depth as they were in their nursery beds (see p.216 for planting tips).

START PRUNING APPLE AND PEAR TREES after leaf-fall, taking out dead and diseased wood and crossing stems, plus some older branches, removing about 20 per cent of the existing canopy to produce an open framework that will allow light into the centre of the plant.

TURN THE COMPOST by taking out what's in your bin and then putting it all back. The additional air you will have introduced encourages faster composting.

PRUNE GOOSEBERRIES AND REDCURRANTS. Shorten all side-shoots to one to three buds from the base, and cut back the tips of the main branches by 25 per cent to an outward-facing bud. Also remove any dead or diseased shoots.

PRUNING YOUNG BLACKCURRANT BUSHES. For the first three years after planting, prune lightly in autumn or winter if growth is strong, just removing any weak or low-lying shoots. If stems look spindly or are unproductive, prune hard, cutting back one in three shoots to near ground level each winter, targeting the oldest shoots.

Indoors

MONITOR THE TEMPERATURE, ensuring that houseplants are not exposed to cold conditions, especially at night, by removing them from draughty windowsills, and checking any kept in unheated rooms.

PLANT HIPPEASTRUMS now, setting them in pots of peat-free multipurpose compost, with the top two-thirds of the bulb above the surface. Water sparingly until the leaves appear. Keep at 21°C (70°F) until they flower, usually 6–8 weeks after planting, then move to a cooler room, no lower than 15°C (60°F), to extend the blooming period. Turn the pot every few days to prevent the stems leaning towards the light.

Plant now

1. Bare-root deciduous trees (such as hornbeam)
2. Yew (*Taxus baccata*)
3. Elephant's ears (*Bergenia* species)
4. Darwin's berberis (*Berberis darwinii*)
5. Dogwood (*Cornus alba*)
6. Japanese aralia (*Fatsia japonica*)
7. Witch hazel (such as *Hamamelis × intermedia*)
8. Lily turf (*Liriope muscari*)
9. Black mondo grass (*Ophiopogon planiscapus* 'Nigrescens')
10. Roses (*Rosa*)
11. Tulips (*Tulipa*)

Project: Plant a bare-root fruit tree

The first bare-root fruit trees are available in November, which is also the best time to plant them. These trees are grown in a field and when dormant from late autumn to early spring, they're dug up and sold with the roots wrapped in hessian or similar material.

Specialist nurseries offer a wide choice of bare-root fruit trees, from young whips just a couple of years old to larger, more mature specimens. Check that the tree will enjoy the soil and light conditions in your garden, asking the nursery for advice on suitable choices if you're not sure.

When your tree arrives, you can store it for a few days in a cold, frost-free shed or garage, but then plant it as soon as possible after that. If the ground is frozen or waterlogged, unwrap your tree and plant it temporarily in a large pot of compost until the soil conditions improve. After planting, frosty ground will be no problem for these hardy trees.

To plant, dig a square hole three times as wide and the same depth as the root ball, so that once planted the tree will be at the same level in the soil as it was before it was dug up; a dark mark on the stem will guide you. Also remove grass and other plants from around the root area. Do not include any organic matter or compost, which may cause the tree to sink once planted. There is also no need to add any fertilizer at the planting stage. Backfill with the excavated soil, firming it around the trunk, then apply a 5–8cm (2–3in) layer of bark chips (mulch) over the soil, leaving a 10cm (4in) gap around the trunk.

Young trees will not require a stake but taller specimens may need one. Hammer in a stake; it should meet the tree one third of the way up the trunk, with at least 60cm (2ft) driven into the ground. Secure the stake to the tree with a tree tie, and check it every year, loosening as necessary; remove after two or three years when the roots are established.

The tree will benefit enormously from watering in thoroughly as the soil is backfilled, but then will not need watering until spring After that, make sure to keep the roots moist during dry spells for two to three years. Also keep an area of 1m (3ft) in diameter around the tree clear of grass and other vegetation, and ask your supplier about pruning requirements for your chosen variety.

Looking up

Sunrise and Sunset

The hours of daylight for planting and pruning are getting shorter in November, so check the weather forecast and plan as many activities as you can for fine, sunny days.

	LONDON		EDINBURGH	
	Sunrise	Sunset	Sunrise	Sunset
Fri, Nov 1	6:53:16 am	4:34:52 pm	7:18:47 am	4:33:51 pm
Sat, Nov 2	6:55:02 am	4:33:06 pm	7:20:54 am	4:31:42 pm
Sun, Nov 3	6:56:47 am	4:31:21 pm	7:23:01 am	4:29:36 pm
Mon, Nov 4	6:58:32 am	4:29:37 pm	7:25:07 am	4:27:31 pm
Tue, Nov 5	7:00:18 am	4:27:55 pm	7:27:14 am	4:25:28 pm
Wed, Nov 6	7:02:03 am	4:26:16 pm	7:29:20 am	4:23:27 pm
Thu, Nov 7	7:03:48 am	4:24:37 pm	7:31:26 am	4:21:28 pm
Fri, Nov 8	7:05:32 am	4:23:01 pm	7:33:32 am	4:19:31 pm
Sat, Nov 9	7:07:17 am	4:21:27 pm	7:35:38 am	4:17:35 pm
Sun, Nov 10	7:09:01 am	4:19:55 pm	7:37:43 am	4:15:42 pm
Mon, Nov 11	7:10:45 am	4:18:25 pm	7:39:48 am	4:13:51 pm
Tue, Nov 12	7:12:28 am	4:16:56 pm	7:41:52 am	4:12:02 pm
Wed, Nov 13	7:14:11 am	4:15:30 pm	7:43:55 am	4:10:16 pm
Thu, Nov 14	7:15:54 am	4:14:07 pm	7:45:58 am	4:08:32 pm
Fri, Nov 15	7:17:36 am	4:12:45 pm	7:48:01 am	4:06:50 pm
Sat, Nov 16	7:19:17 am	4:11:26 pm	7:50:02 am	4:05:10 pm
Sun, Nov 17	7:20:58 am	4:10:09 pm	7:52:03 am	4:03:34 pm
Mon, Nov 18	7:22:37 am	4:08:55 pm	7:54:02 am	4:02:00 pm
Tue, Nov 19	7:24:16 am	4:07:43 pm	7:56:01 am	4:00:28 pm
Wed, Nov 20	7:25:54 am	4:06:34 pm	7:57:58 am	3:59:00 pm
Thu, Nov 21	7:27:32 am	4:05:27 pm	7:59:54 am	3:57:34 pm
Fri, Nov 22	7:29:08 am	4:04:23 pm	8:01:49 am	3:56:11 pm
Sat, Nov 23	7:30:42 am	4:03:22 pm	8:03:42 am	3:54:51 pm
Sun, Nov 24	7:32:16 am	4:02:23 pm	8:05:34 am	3:53:35 pm
Mon, Nov 25	7:33:48 am	4:01:27 pm	8:07:24 am	3:52:21 pm
Tue, Nov 26	7:35:19 am	4:00:34 pm	8:09:12 am	3:51:11 pm
Wed, Nov 27	7:36:49 am	3:59:44 pm	8:10:59 am	3:50:04 pm
Thu, Nov 28	7:38:17 am	3:58:57 pm	8:12:43 am	3:49:00 pm
Fri, Nov 29	7:39:43 am	3:58:13 pm	8:14:26 am	3:48:00 pm
Sat, Nov 30	7:41:08 am	3:57:32 pm	8:16:06 am	3:47:04 pm

Moonrise and moonset

Moon Phases

● **NEW MOON** 1 November   ○ **FULL MOON** 15 November
◑ **FIRST QUARTER** 9 November   ◐ **THIRD QUARTER** 23 November

MONTH	LONDON			EDINBURGH		
	Moonrise	Moonset	Moonrise	Moonrise	Moonset	Moonrise
1	06:56	16:08		07:26	16:02	
2	08:11	16:25		08:48	16:12	
3	09:27	16:49		10:12	16:28	
4	10:40	17:23		11:33	16:55	
5	11:45	18:11		12:41	17:40	
6	12:36	19:15		13:30	18:47	
7	13:14	20:32		14:01	20:12	
8	13:41	21:56		14:19	21:44	
9	14:00	23:22		14:31	23:19	
10	14:15			14:39		
11	-	00:49	14:29	-	00:53	14:46
12	-	02:16	14:41	-	02:27	14:52
13	-	03:44	14:54	-	04:03	14:58
14	-	05:16	15:10	-	05:42	15:07
15	-	06:50	15:30	-	07:25	15:19
16	-	08:25	15:59	-	09:10	15:39
17	-	09:53	16:41	-	10:46	16:13
18	-	11:05	17:40	-	12:01	17:10
19	-	11:57	18:53	-	12:48	18:28
20	-	12:31	20:13	-	13:15	19:56
21	-	12:55	21:32	-	13:30	21:24
22	-	13:11	22:49	-	13:40	22:47
23	-	13:24		-	13:46	
24	00:01	13:34		00:06	13:51	
25	01:12	13:44		01:22	13:56	
26	02:21	13:53		02:37	14:00	
27	03:31	14:03		03:52	14:05	
28	04:42	14:15		05:10	14:11	
29	05:57	14:31		06:31	14:20	
30	07:13	14:53		07:55	14:34	

Average rainfall

One of the wettest months of the year, the 20-year average rainfall for the UK in November is 147mm (5.8in). Since the growth of most plants is slow at this time of year, you are unlikely to need to irrigate them now.

LOCATION	DAYS	MM	INCHES
Aberdeen	15	93	3.7
Aberystwyth	18	123	4.8
Belfast	16	102	4.0
Birmingham	13	79	3.1
Bournemouth	14	108	4.3
Bristol	15	90	3.5
Cambridge	10	53	2.0
Canterbury	11	75	3.0
Cardiff	16	131	5.2
Edinburgh	12	65	2.6
Exeter	16	155	6.1
Glasgow	17	132	5.2
Gloucester	14	89	3.5
Inverness	13	67	2.6
Ipswich	11	55	2.2
Leeds	16	109	4.3
Liverpool	15	82	3.2
London	12	76	3.0
Manchester	17	124	4.9
Newcastle upon Tyne	12	70	2.8
Norwich	13	71	2.8
Nottingham	13	69	2.7
Oxford	12	71	2.8
Sheffield	13	85	3.3
Truro	18	128	5.0

Reuse and reduce plastics

We are all now aware, more than ever before, that reducing the use of plastics in the garden is good for the environment. Most plastics are made from non-renewable sources, such as oil, and they take a long time to break down in the environment, while also releasing tiny particles, or microplastics, in the process.

While we all want to reduce our use of plastic, buying new alternatives is often not as sustainable as reusing the plastic items we already have. And where there is no alternative to buying new, consider whether the products will break down naturally (such as bamboo, coir or jute) or can be recycled commercially and placed in kerb-side collection bins or taken to a recycling centre.

POTS, CONTAINERS AND TRAYS

From takeaway cartons to Christmas sweet tubs, most of us have plastic containers that we can reuse for storing seeds, hand tools and gardening sundries. Washed and stored out of sunlight, they often last for decades. Foil and plastic food trays, plastic cups and yoghurt pots can be used for seed sowing – just pierce a few drainage holes in the base. Hard plastics can be difficult to recycle, so reuse is the best option.

COMPOST BAGS

It's hard to avoid buying products such as compost and soil improvers in plastic bags. However, these can be used again. They are ideal for lining containers and baskets to reduce evaporation and can also be weighted down to cover and smother difficult weeds such as ground elder. A few suppliers are beginning to offer a 'bag for life', allowing you to refill them at garden centres, but this service isn't widely available. Although they're not widely recycled, some garden centres are now accepting old compost bags for recycling, too.

PLASTIC BOTTLES

Creative gardeners have led the way in finding uses for household items, such as plastic milk and soft drinks bottles. Cutting the bottom off gives you a mini cloche that can be used to protect young seedlings in early spring; take off the top for additional ventilation and they can be stacked and stored in a shed without taking up much space.

Alternatively, if you pierce the lid of a plastic bottle multiple times and fill it with water, you can make a mini watering can with a fine spray, ideal for watering established seedlings.

NETTING AND SUPPORT

Plastic-free netting, often made from jute, is becoming more widely available, or you could try making your own from string, if you have the patience – but do reuse old plastic netting if you have it, rather than throwing it away. Instead of buying bamboo canes and hazel poles, you could grow these plants in your garden and harvest the stems – cutting them regularly will also help to manage the size of these potentially large plants.

Edible garden

November is a busy time for storing and preserving fruits harvested last month, and picking hardy autumn crops that sail through cold, frosty weather.

Veg in season

SWEDES AND PARSNIPS are hardier than other root crops such as turnips and potatoes and able to cope with colder soil, so leave these in the ground through winter until you are ready to use them. **1**

SALAD LEAVES including rocket and lettuces sown late in summer will be ready to pick now, and may offer a crop until late in the month if protected by a cloche. **2**

KALE PROVIDES FRESH VITAMIN-RICH LEAVES at this time of year, but you may need to net your crops to protect them from pigeons. **3**

PULL LEEKS sown in spring and planted out in early summer. **4**

Fruit in season

THE LAST OF THE APPLES AND PEARS will be ready to pick early in the month; you can then store them for use over winter (see p.202).

FEELING ADVENTUROUS? Pineberries are essentially white strawberries that have a distinctive pineapple-like flavour. Plant them in autumn or spring, in a sunny spot and free-draining soil. Pineberries flower in May and need a pollination partner such as a regular strawberry plant for the white fruits with dark red seeds to develop. Remove the flowers in the first year to allow plants to build up a strong root system for future years' crops. The fruit will be ready to harvest in June the year after planting, and because birds do not recognize them, your crop won't need netting. Protect the leaves and stems with straw over winter.

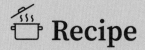

Recipe

ROOT AND BEAN STEW

This simple recipe uses up your freshly harvested root crops and makes a warming dish for lunchtime or a simple evening meal. The ingredients here are for guidance and you can add any vegetables you fancy that are ready to pick now. It is important to use baking or roasting potatoes which will create a thick stew as they break down during the cooking process, but do not cut them into tiny chunks or they will dissolve completely.

1 Fry the onion in the olive oil in a large saucepan, then add the potatoes. Cover the potatoes and onion with water and bring to the boil, then add the stock cubes, turmeric, curry powder, chilli and carrots, and simmer for 15 minutes.

2 Stir in the cabbage and bring back to the boil, making sure all the ingredients are mixed well and covered with liquid. Simmer for a further 10 minutes, until the vegetables are cooked.

3 Add the garlic cloves, tomatoes and beans and heat through, stirring the stew to prevent it burning. Simmer gently for about 5 minutes, then turn off the heat. Serve with crusty or wholemeal bread.

INGREDIENTS

1 large onion, finely chopped
2 tbsp olive oil
4 large potatoes, cut into large chunks
2 vegetable stock cubes
1 tsp turmeric
1 tsp curry powder
I dried chilli
6 large carrots, sliced
Half a cabbage, finely chopped
2 cloves garlic
400g (14oz) can chopped tomatoes
395g (14oz) can mixed beans
A few fresh rosemary leaves, chopped

Challenges of the month

November is usually too cold for fungal diseases to spread, but some may linger in milder autumns. Invertebrates are less likely to cause problems as winter approaches.

CLUB ROOT causes the roots of cabbages, Brussels sprouts, turnips and other brassicas to swell and become distorted, leading to stunted and poor growth above the ground. To prevent infection, buy club-root resistant cultivars. If your crops have been affected by the disease in the past, try growing them in pots so that they reach a larger size with a healthy root system before transplanting them, which may help them to resist attack in contaminated ground. You can also minimize the risk by adding lime to raise the pH of soil – follow the instructions on the packaging. Improving the soil drainage and growing crops in raised beds if you garden on clay will also help.

TULIP VIRUSES can infect tulips and cause streaks in the colours of the flowers when they open in spring, as well as brown streaks or mottled colours on the leaves and stems. To prevent these viruses, check your bulbs carefully before planting and discard any with sunken brown spots, arcs or rings. You can also lower the risk of infection by buying your bulbs from a reputable source and destroying any affected plants to prevent the virus spreading.

FIREBLIGHT is a bacterial disease that makes affected trees and shrubs look like they have been scorched by fire, hence the name. Apples, pears and other plants in the Rosaceae family, such as *Cotoneaster, Sorbus, Crataegus* (hawthorn), *Photinia* and *Pyracantha*, are susceptible. A slimy white liquid may exude from infections in wet weather, and new shoots shrivel and die as the infection spreads, while the wood beneath the bark becomes stained a reddish-brown colour. You may also see areas of dead, sunken bark (cankers) on branches of infected shoots. Prune out and burn infected stems and branches as soon as you identify them, cutting back 30cm (1ft) beyond the stained wood in smaller branches, and 60cm (2ft) in larger branches. Wipe the soil from pruning tools and apply a garden disinfectant between cuts to avoid spreading the bacteria. Remove secondary, late blossoms before they open.

Look out for

The wood mouse

A common resident of gardens throughout the UK, the tiny wood or field mouse (*Apodemus sylvaticus*) can sometimes be seen scurrying about in November searching for food. Unlike the house mouse, which seeks shelter in the warmth of your home at this time of year, the shy wood mouse remains in the garden, sheltering in a burrow underground or in another place that's protected from the worst of the weather and predators such as cats, foxes and owls.

The little brown wood mouse looks similar to its house-dwelling cousin, with a golden-brown coat and long tail, but it has larger ears and eyes relative to its size. It does not hibernate and is mostly nocturnal, but you may see this agile creature at dusk climbing stems to reach juicy berries or nutritious seeds, some of which will be stored for later in its burrow or a disused bird's nest. Other favourite foods include fruit, fungi, snails and insects, so while these little mice may nibble small holes in your apples and pears, they also help to keep a balance in the garden ecosystem.

Female wood mice can have up to six litters a year, usually between February and October, giving birth in their burrows to between four and eight pups, which are hairless, with closed eyes and ears. The babies feed on their mother's milk for about three weeks before they are able to search for their own food. They become sexually active after two months, and most wood mice live for less than a year. Take care when digging around sheds or outbuildings where these little rodents are most likely to make their burrows.

Identifying Ornamental Grasses

No garden is complete without a few ornamental grasses, which decorate the autumn garden with stems of feathery seedheads or colourful leaves. Most are fully hardy, but some may suffer in cold spots, so check labels before buying. The best choices for seedhead interest in November include the feather reed grass (*Calamagrostis*), pampas grass (*Cortaderia*), eulalia (*Miscanthus*), switch grass (*Panicum*) and the fountain grasses (*Pennisetum*). Plant in moist but free-draining soil and sun and cut back deciduous grasses in early spring to make way for new growth.

PAMPAS GRASS (*CORTADERIA SELLOANA* 'PUMILA' AGM)
An evergreen grass, 'Pumila' is a good pampas for a small garden, producing a fountain of arching dark green leaves and silky creamy-white plumes from late summer.
H x S: 1.5 x 1.2m (5 x 4ft)

EULALIA (*MISCANTHUS SINENSIS* 'KLEINE SILBERSPINNE' AGM)
A compact eulalia, 'Kleine Silberspinne' has arching, silvery leaves with white midribs, and feathery reddish flowerheads followed by pale brown seedheads.
H x S: 1.2 x 0.45m (4ft x 18in)

FOUNTAIN GRASS (*PENNISETUM ALOPECUROIDES* 'HAMELN' AGM)
Forming a low mound of slim green leaves that turn yellow then brown over winter, this grass's pinkish-white, bottle-brush-like flowerheads turn paler in colour when the seeds form.
H x S: 1.2 x 1m (4ft x 3ft)

SWITCH GRASS (*PANICUM VIRGATUM* 'HEAVY METAL' AGM)
Ideal for a small, sunny border, the upright, metallic blue-grey leaves of this switch grass turn yellow in autumn, when spikes of tiny purple-green flowers also appear.
H x S: 1.5 x 0.75m (5ft x 2ft 6in)

FEATHER REED GRASS (*CALAMAGROSTIS* × *ACUTIFLORA* 'KARL FOERSTER' AGM)
This popular grass forms a compact clump of tall, upright green leaves, with wands of green flowers in summer that turn buff-coloured as the seedheads develop.
H x S: 1.8 x 0.6m (6 x2ft)

Garden tales

Orchids have long been treasured for their exquisite flower shapes and colours, and while some are challenging to grow at home, the moth orchid (*Phalaenopsis*) can bloom for months with the minimum of care. We can now pick up one of these beauties for just a few pounds from the supermarket, but when they were first discovered in the 1800s, plant hunters were prepared to risk their lives for the eye-watering prices the precious flowers commanded.

Wealthy Victorians spent fortunes buying and growing the exotic blooms in expensive glass-fronted, heated rooms, with limited success. They also financed individual plant hunters and companies to search for new species in far-away lands. Dubbed 'orchidelirium', or 'orchidomania', the craze for these flowers spurred fierce competition among the hunters and traders. Pursuing these rare plants was a dangerous game, and many were killed by disease, accidents, and even fellow plant hunters. Stories also spread about unscrupulous men who took money from their clients, holidayed in Europe on the proceeds, and then brought back common orchids that were widely available and could be bought for the lowest price.

As time went on, knowledge about orchids and how to grow them increased, and in 1851 B.S. Williams published his book *The Orchid Grower's Manual*, which helped to educate owners about their care. Botanists also learned how to propagate the plants and, as a result, prices started to fall as more were bred at home.

Today, rare orchids are still highly prized and profits from the illegal trade puts them at risk of being stolen. Trading in orchids harvested from the wild is banned by the Convention on International Trade in Endangered Species of Wild Fauna and Flora (CITES), with a few exemptions and strict conditions, but this has not deterred smugglers from removing many threatened species. Even those grown at botanic gardens such as Kew in London are not safe and have to be guarded by 24-hour camera surveillance equipment and security staff, while the rarest species are displayed in locked glass cabinets.

Legend: The mighty oak

Our native oak (*Quercus*) has been revered throughout history, earning the title 'mighty' due to its size, strength and longevity. Sacred to many people, from the ancient Greeks and Romans to the Scandinavians and Celts, it's also the national tree of England and Wales and is still worshipped to this day.

As one of the tallest trees in a forest, the oak is often struck by lightning, but frequently survives the ordeal, regenerating afterwards and continuing to thrive. This power over nature led to the tree's association with the kings of the gods in many mythologies, including Jupiter and Zeus, the Roman and Greek gods of the sky and thunder, and the Norse god Thor, who held the same title.

The ancient Celts viewed the oak as a symbol of strength and wisdom, and the Druids held religious ceremonies in oak forests – the word Druid is thought to mean 'knower of the oak tree'.

When Christianity came to Britain, worship of the oak continued. Saint Brendan was inspired by God to use oak boards instead of animal hides to build his coracle, which legend says carried him to America hundreds of years before Columbus. Robin Hood and his Merry Men were also said to have climbed the Major Oak in Sherwood Forest to plot their raids against the rich and Sheriff of Nottingham in safety – that oak still survives today and is thought to be one thousand years old.

In the Middle Ages, many parishes designated one tree as the Gospel Oak, where the Gospel was read out during the Beating of the Bounds ceremonies at Rogantide in spring, a tradition that lasted until the 19th century.

It was also among the branches of an oak that King Charles II hid from the Roundheads at Boscobel, and in 1660 he made the 29th May 'Royal Oak Day' to celebrate the restoration of the monarchy. Children wore oak leaves and oak apples during the festivities, and while the holiday, also known as Oak Apple Day, was abolished in 1859, the tradition continues today in some parts of the country.

December

Midwinter, and the garden sleeps like a fairy-tale princess beneath a veil of ice. Herbaceous plants have taken refuge underground, only their roots surviving beneath the brown earth, and the bony fingers of deciduous trees reach up in prayer to the cold, milky sky. Oaks are among the last to release their leafy hoard, revealing intricate canopies, while the magpie's castanet call breaks the silent dawn.

KEY EVENTS

Winter Solstice (shortest day of the year), 21 December
Christmas Day, 25 December
First Day of Hanukkah, 26 December
New Year's Eve, 31 December

What to do

The inclement winter weather may prevent us from gardening in December, but the pause in activity offers a time for reflection and forward planning. Bare-root trees, shrubs and roses are still available and will be ready to plant as soon as they arrive, if the ground is not frozen or waterlogged (see p.212 and p.214). You can also prune fruit trees now (see p.214) and insulate garden taps, hoses and pipes at the beginning of the month, if you have not already done so.

In the garden

SWEEP UP THE LAST OF THE FALLEN TREE LEAVES from lawns, paths and patios, and scoop them out of ponds and small water features if you have not netted them (see p.192). **1**

CONTINUE TO FEED THE BIRDS and put out fresh water, particularly when ponds and water features are frozen over. **2**

ORDER SEEDS AND PLANTS for delivery in the New Year or later in spring. Do it now because there is little time to make detailed plans when the sowing and planting season begins in spring and taking advantage of this quiet time can pay dividends.

PRUNE CLIMBING ROSES that are at risk of wind-rock, when their long, tall stems are blown about and dislodge the root ball. After removing dead and diseased wood, cut back new side-stems formed this year to a few buds from the older main stems and tie them into their supports. On established plants, cut a few of the oldest stems back to near ground level to encourage new shoots to develop. **3**

BRUSH SNOW FROM HEDGES and shrubs that may break under the weight. **4**

PLACE ALL POTTED PLANTS ON POT FEET or bricks to raise them off the ground where they risk standing in puddles, which could lead to waterlogged compost and, potentially, root rot (see p.185).

In the fruit & veg patch

CHECK TREE TIES on trees planted in the previous 12 months and loosen as necessary.

SOW MICROGREENS in pots indoors for a steady supply of fresh nutrient-rich leaves (see p.14).

EARTH UP BRUSSELS SPROUT STEMS to stabilize them in windy weather and remove yellow leaves regularly as they may harbour fungal diseases if left on the ground.

PRUNE YOUNG BLACKCURRANT BUSHES. For the first three years after planting, prune lightly in autumn or winter if growth is strong, removing only thin, weak stems or those growing close to the ground. If growth is weak, prune harder, cutting up to half the stems back to the base of the plant.

Indoors

TENDER AZALEAS (*Rhododendron simsii* cultivars) brighten up indoor winter displays and are available now in a range of jewel colours. To maintain them, make sure the compost is consistently moist, but not waterlogged, and keep them in a cool but sunny spot, such as a windowsill in a hallway or in a conservatory.

MOVE FORCED HYACINTH BULBS into a warm room (but not too hot) when shoots appear, in order to encourage flowering over the festive period.

Plant now

1. Bare-root trees (such as *Acer palmatum* 'Orange Dream')
2. Bare-root deciduous shrubs (such as *Hypericum*)
3. Coral bark willow (*Salix alba* var. *vitellina* 'Britzensis')
4. Skimmia (*Skimmia japonica*)
5. Laurustinus (*Viburnum tinus* 'Eve Price' AGM)
6. Holly (*Ilex* species)
7. Winter heather (*Erica carnea* and *E. darleyensis*)
8. Foam flower (*Tiarella cordifolia*)
9. Sedge (*Carex* species)
10. Japanese pink pussy willow (*Salix gracilistyla* 'Mount Aso')
11. Ghost bramble (*Rubus thibetanus* AGM)

Project: Natural winter wreath

Make a sustainable wreath to decorate your door during the festive season, using the foliage from the garden and foraged berries and cones. First, purchase a metal wreath frame from a floristry supplier that will fit your doorframe once covered with foliage, which will roughly double its size. Also buy a reel of florist's wire or strong green garden twine, and a bag of sustainably sourced carpet moss. If you can't find moss, you can use straw instead but it will not retain as much moisture, so your wreath may not last as long. You will also need a selection of evergreen leafy stems – bay, ivy, pine, viburnum and camellia are good choices. Also cut from the garden or forage a selection of holly berries, rose hips, crab apples and pine cones.

Start by covering the metal frame with a thick layer of moss, securing it well with the florist's wire or string. Then cut each of the leafy stems to about 15–20cm (6–8in) in length, and crush the base with a hammer before plunging them into water for about 30 minutes to soak up the moisture.

Take your first stem and lay it on the moss base at a slight angle, securing it with wire or string. Lay the second stem next to it, so that the leaves overlap the base of the first one, and secure it to the frame. Continue in this way until the whole frame is covered with foliage. Now add your berries, hips and pine cones to create a colourful wreath, twisting wire around the stems and cones to secure them in place. You can also use small eating apples if you don't have many berries or cones in the garden.

Using a double length of wire or string, make a loop at the top of the wreath to hang it on your door. The metal frame can be used year after year, while all the other natural elements can be added to the compost heap or put in the green waste at your local recycling centre.

Looking up

Sunrise and Sunset

December's short days and winter weather leave little time for gardening, but you can use the time to clear out the shed, and plan your crops and flowers for next year.

	LONDON		EDINBURGH	
	Sunrise	Sunset	Sunrise	Sunset
Sun, Dec 1	7:42:31 am	3:56:54 pm	8:17:44 am	3:46:11 pm
Mon, Dec 2	7:43:52 am	3:56:19 pm	8:19:19 am	3:45:21 pm
Tue, Dec 3	7:45:11 am	3:55:48 pm	8:20:52 am	3:44:36 pm
Wed, Dec 4	7:46:28 am	3:55:19 pm	8:22:23 am	3:43:54 pm
Thu, Dec 5	7:47:43 am	3:54:54 pm	8:23:50 am	3:43:16 pm
Fri, Dec 6	7:48:55 am	3:54:32 pm	8:25:15 am	3:42:42 pm
Sat, Dec 7	7:50:06 am	3:54:14 pm	8:26:37 am	3:42:12 pm
Sun, Dec 8	7:51:14 am	3:53:58 pm	8:27:56 am	3:41:46 pm
Mon, Dec 9	7:52:19 am	3:53:47 pm	8:29:12 am	3:41:24 pm
Tue, Dec 10	7:53:22 am	3:53:38 pm	8:30:24 am	3:41:06 pm
Wed, Dec 11	7:54:23 am	3:53:33 pm	8:31:33 am	3:40:52 pm
Thu, Dec 12	7:55:20 am	3:53:31 pm	8:32:39 am	3:40:43 pm
Fri, Dec 13	7:56:15 am	3:53:33 pm	8:33:41 am	3:40:37 pm
Sat, Dec 14	7:57:08 am	3:53:38 pm	8:34:39 am	3:40:36 pm
Sun, Dec 15	7:57:57 am	3:53:46 pm	8:35:34 am	3:40:39 pm
Mon, Dec 16	7:58:43 am	3:53:58 pm	8:36:25 am	3:40:46 pm
Tue, Dec 17	7:59:27 am	3:54:13 pm	8:37:12 am	3:40:58 pm
Wed, Dec 18	8:00:07 am	3:54:32 pm	8:37:56 am	3:41:13 pm
Thu, Dec 19	8:00:45 am	3:54:54 pm	8:38:35 am	3:41:33 pm
Fri, Dec 20	8:01:19 am	3:55:19 pm	8:39:10 am	3:41:57 pm
Sat, Dec 21	8:01:50 am	3:55:48 pm	8:39:42 am	3:42:26 pm
Sun, Dec 22	8:02:18 am	3:56:20 pm	8:40:09 am	3:42:58 pm
Mon, Dec 23	8:02:42 am	3:56:55 pm	8:40:32 am	3:43:35 pm
Tue, Dec 24	8:03:04 am	3:57:33 pm	8:40:51 am	3:44:15 pm
Wed, Dec 25	8:03:22 am	3:58:14 pm	8:41:06 am	3:45:00 pm
Thu, Dec 26	8:03:36 am	3:58:59 pm	8:41:16 am	3:45:48 pm
Fri, Dec 27	8:03:48 am	3:59:47 pm	8:41:23 am	3:46:41 pm
Sat, Dec 28	8:03:56 am	4:00:37 pm	8:41:25 am	3:47:37 pm
Sun, Dec 29	8:04:00 am	4:01:31 pm	8:41:23 am	3:48:37 pm
Mon, Dec 30	8:04:02 am	4:02:27 pm	8:41:17 am	3:49:41 pm
Tue, Dec 31	8:04:00 am	4:03:26 pm	8:41:07 am	3:50:48 pm

Moonrise and moonset

Moon Phases

● **NEW MOON** 1 December   ○ **FULL MOON** 15 December
◐ **FIRST QUARTER** 8 December   ◑ **THIRD QUARTER** 22 December

MONTH	LONDON			EDINBURGH		
	Moonrise	Moonset	Moonrise	Moonrise	Moonset	Moonrise
1	08:28	15:23		09:18	14:58	
2	09:36	16:07		10:32	15:37	
3	10:33	17:08		11:28	16:38	
4	11:15	18:22		12:03	17:59	
5	11:44	19:44		12:25	19:30	
6	12:06	21:09		12:38	21:04	
7	12:22	22:34		12:47	22:36	
8	12:35	23:58		12:54		
9	12:47			-	00:07	13:00
10	-	01:22	13:00	-	01:38	13:06
11	-	02:49	13:14	-	03:12	13:14
12	-	04:19	13:31	-	04:50	13:24
13	-	05:51	13:55	-	06:31	13:39
14	-	07:22	14:30	-	08:11	14:06
15	-	08:42	15:20	-	09:37	14:51
16	-	09:44	16:28	-	10:37	16:00
17	-	10:26	17:47	-	11:13	17:27
18	-	10:55	19:09	-	11:34	18:57
19	-	11:15	20:29	-	11:46	20:24
20	-	11:29	21:44	-	11:54	21:47
21	-	11:40	22:56	-	12:00	23:05
22	-	11:50		-	12:04	
23	00:07	12:00		00:20	12:09	
24	01:16	12:10		01:36	12:13	
25	02:27	12:21		02:52	12:19	
26	03:40	12:35		04:12	12:27	
27	04:55	12:54		05:34	12:39	
28	06:11	13:21		06:58	12:58	
29	07:23	14:00		08:17	13:31	
30	08:25	14:56		09:21	14:25	
31	09:13	16:07		10:04	15:42	

Average rainfall

The 20-year average rainfall for the UK in December is 166mm (6.5in), making it equal January as the wettest months of the year. The high rainfall helps to replenish ground water supplies but also increases the risk of flooding this month.

LOCATION	DAYS	MM	INCHES
Aberdeen	13	78	3.0
Aberystwyth	17	127	5.0
Belfast	15	93	3.7
Birmingham	13	84	3.3
Bournemouth	13	104	4.1
Bristol	13	90	3.5
Cambridge	10	49	1.9
Canterbury	12	72	2.8
Cardiff	15	140	5.5
Edinburgh	12	67	2.6
Exeter	17	186	7.3
Glasgow	17	161	6.3
Gloucester	13	85	3.3
Inverness	14	73	2.9
Ipswich	11	57	2.2
Leeds	16	121	4.8
Liverpool	15	92	3.6
London	12	68	2.7
Manchester	18	139	5.5
Newcastle upon Tyne	11	55	2.2
Norwich	13	64	2.5
Nottingham	12	70	2.7
Oxford	12	66	2.6
Sheffield	14	87	3.4
Truro	17	116	4.6

Long live houseplants

Houseplants that have the lowest impact on the environment are those that survive for many years and can be propagated easily to make new plants. To identify a plant's survival prospects, check its requirements on the label, and supplement your knowledge by reading books and researching online. Be alert for plants with sensitivity to low light levels, dry air, temperature variations and overwatering, and select those that are adapted to the conditions in your home.

LIGHT WORK

Flowering plants typically need higher light levels than foliage plants and are often more challenging to keep alive for long periods, while some, such as gardenias and poinsettia, are notably short-lived. However, other trusted favourites, including Christmas cacti, hippeastrums, indoor azaleas and cyclamens, often thrive for years.

Cacti and succulents generally like high light levels, even coping with some direct summer sun, which damages many other houseplants. However, check labels carefully, since 'forest cacti' such as the Christmas and fishbone cactus are tree dwellers and prefer diffused light.

Many foliage houseplants come from tropical forests and have adapted to life beneath the tree canopies. Consequently, they prefer diffused light, away from direct sun. They vary in their resilience to sunlight, though, and those with leathery leaves are generally tougher than plants with more papery foliage that may scorch easily. But while plants such as philodendrons and kentia palms can survive in rooms with low light levels, they will grow better and live longer in a brighter spot. One way to achieve this is to bring your plants outside for a summer sojourn in the garden when the nights are warm enough for them. Place them in light shade and return them to the brightest areas of your house in early autumn before temperatures plummet.

FOOD FOR THOUGHT

Houseplants benefit from feeding during their main growth period, usually from spring to late summer or early autumn. However, fertilizers won't

(leaf stalks), leaf blades or leaf sections. Some, including coleus (*Solenostemon*) and tradescantia, are very easy to propagate by simply putting cut stems in a jar of water. The Mexican hat plant (*Kalanchoe daigremontiana*) and some others sprinkle daughter plants around the parent, which you can remove and pot on to make new plants.

Air layering is useful for 'leggy' woody plants such as ornamental indoor figs (*Ficus*). Using a sharp, clean knife, make a small cut on a healthy stem, without severing it. Then surround the wounded area with a plastic sleeve filled with sphagnum moss. Seal the sleeve at the top and bottom and leave for several months until plant roots develop from the wound. You can then cut off the stem with the roots attached and pot it on.

Propagate your plants from May to September, which will allow new plants to develop good roots before winter.

compensate for insufficient light or warmth, which will inhibit growth, and if your conditions are not completely favourable and growth is slow, your plants will not need as much food.

Most shop-bought houseplants are grown in peat-based potting compost, but special peat-free composts are also available. Use these to repot congested plants, ideally in spring, to support root health and promote growth and longevity.

MAKING MORE PLANTS
In their native forests, houseplants take root readily to produce new plants. At home, many also root freely from stem cuttings, tubers, rhizomes, petioles

Edible garden

December is a great month for harvesting winter crops such as sprouts, cabbages, carrots, parsnips and swedes, while stored squash and white and red cabbages provide more home-grown ingredients over the festive period.

Veg in season

BRUSSELS SPROUTS AND CABBAGE are hardy plants that stand strong throughout bitter winter conditions. For a long harvest and sweeter crops, leave sprouts in the ground until frosted and then start picking the firm ones on the lower part of the stem, pulling them off by tugging them downwards. **1**

ROOT CROPS including swedes, turnips, carrots, and celeriac continue to provide a harvest in December. **2**

PARSNIPS are now at their peak, the cold weather having induced the release of sugars to sweeten these delicious seasonal favourites.

Fruit in season

STORED TREE FRUITS such as apples and pears will still be good to eat in December, while preserves and frozen berries offer a taste of summer in the depths of winter.

FEELING ADVENTUROUS? If you're looking for vitamin-rich berries and live in a mild region, try growing sea buckthorn (*Hippophae rhamnoides*). This decorative Mediterranean shrub produces thorny stems of silvery foliage and in summer and early autumn bright orange, edible berries appear, which are packed with Vitamin C and taste like lemons. Sea buckthorn grows best in free-draining soil and needs a sheltered, sunny site to thrive. You also require a male and female plant for the fruit to develop but you can save money by buying bare-root shrubs now. Once established, sea buckthorns are easy to care for – just prune them in winter to keep them in check. However, do not plant these shrubs if you live in Ireland, where they are considered a non-native invasive species. **3**

🍲 Recipe

NUT ROAST

This rich nut loaf makes a wonderful vegetarian substitute for a festive turkey lunch and you can simply add more olive oil to replace the butter and use vegan cheese for guests who do not eat any animal products. It will also use up some of your stored carrots, onions and garlic.

1   Heat the oven to 180°C (350°F/Gas 4) and line the base and sides of a 1.5 litre (2lb) loaf tin with parchment paper. Heat the olive oil and butter in a large frying pan and cook the onion, leek, carrot and garlic for about 10 minutes until soft.

2   Stir in the chestnut mushrooms, chestnuts, nuts, cranberries, breadcrumbs and stock and cook for a further 10 minutes. Then add the oregano and paprika and heat through for about a minute.

3   Add the cooked red lentils and tomato purée and cook for a further minute. Then pour in the vegetable stock and simmer over a very gentle heat for about 25 minutes until all the liquid has been absorbed and the mixture is fairly dry. Set aside to cool slightly.

4   When cooled, fold in the beaten eggs, cheddar cheese (if using), parsley and salt and pepper to taste. Spoon the mixture into the prepared tin and press down the surface with the back of the spoon.

5   Cover with foil and bake for 30 minutes, then remove the foil and bake for a further 20 minutes until firm when pressed gently. Allow the loaf to cool in the tin, then turn it out on to a plate. Serve with warm tomato or pasta sauce.

INGREDIENTS

1 tbsp olive oil
15g (½oz) butter
1 large onion, finely chopped
½ leek, finely sliced
1 large carrot, diced
3 cloves of garlic, finely chopped
100g (3½oz) chestnut mushrooms, finely chopped
180g (6½oz) vacuum-packed cooked chestnuts, roughly chopped
150g (5oz) mixed nuts, roughly chopped
30g (1oz) dried cranberries, or apricots, chopped
100g (3½oz) fresh breadcrumbs
300ml (0.6pt) vegetable stock
1 tsp dried oregano
1 tsp smoked paprika
100g (3½oz) red lentils, pre-cooked
2 tbsp tomato purée
300ml (0.5 pint) vegetable stock
3 large eggs, lightly beaten
100g (3½oz) mature cheddar cheese, grated (optional)
Handful flat-leaf parsley, finely chopped

Challenges of the month

As plant growth slows, frosts and low temperatures keep fungal diseases at bay throughout December, while plant-eating invertebrates are hibernating or have died off, posing little risk to outdoor plants. However, indoor plants are still susceptible to illness or stress in winter, so check them regularly and take action quickly.

WITCHES' BROOM looks like a tangle of stems or a large birds' nest in a tree canopy. It may be there all year round but becomes more visible when the tree loses its leaves. The deformity is known as a virescence, but despite the name it is not always due to a virus. In fact, there are multiple causes for a witches' broom to form, and fungi, bacteria and, occasionally, insects may be to blame. The good news is that these growths rarely harm the tree or reduce fruit crops, so they can just be tolerated.

SCALE INSECTS can attack houseplants at any time of year, including winter. They look like little waxy-coated shells and cling to the stems and leaves of a wide variety of indoor plants, sucking the sap from their hosts and leading to distorted growth. Some secrete a sugary honeydew on which sooty moulds can develop. They also lay their eggs under a white fluffy substance in early summer. Healthy plants can tolerate a light infestation, so try to remove the pests as soon as you see the eggs, juvenile nymphs or adults to prevent a more severe attack. The nematode *Steinernema feltiae* is sold as a biological control, but its effectiveness is questionable.

GLASSHOUSE MEALYBUGS are often mistaken for scale insects and suck sap from houseplants in the same way, while their honeydew can also cause sooty moulds to develop. They look like tiny woodlice and are usually covered by a fluffy white wax. To prevent an attack, inspect new plants for signs of mealybugs before buying, and check existing plants regularly, removing the adults and eggs as soon as you see them. You can also put new plants in quarantine before you introduce them to the house, if you are concerned. Biological controls include parasitic wasps (*Leptomastix*, *Leptomastidea* and *Anagrus* species) and may offer some control where mealybug populations are fairly low.

Look out for

The robin

The robin is the undisputed star of winter, for Christmas would not be complete without cards and festive gifts decorated with Britain's best-loved bird. The red breast and little round body of the robin (*Erithacus rubecula*) make it one of our most recognizable native birds, and its association with the winter festivities began in the Victorian era when postmen wore red waistcoats and were nicknamed robins.

Loved for its inquisitive nature, the robin will follow us fearlessly around the garden, seizing worms uncovered as we dig and charming its way into our hearts. But while we cherish these beautiful birds, others may take a different view. Fiercely territorial, robins drive off competitors who dare to breach their boundaries and send out warnings by singing loudly from conspicuous perches.

Robins are widespread throughout Britain. Most gardens are home to one, but not all are year-round residents in the UK – some fly in during the winter from Scandinavia, Europe and Russia to escape the hostile weather in their homelands.

Male and female birds look identical, with a brown back, white belly and red breast and face. In spring and summer, you may see the fledglings with their speckled gold and brown plumage, which gradually takes on the red colouring as they mature.

The breeding season starts in March, but birds may pair up earlier in the year. During this time, the male allows the female to enter his territory, and she then builds a cup-shaped nest among tree roots, shrubs and climbers such as ivy. The female typically lays four to six eggs, which hatch after about 13 days. Both parents brood and feed the chicks, which fledge at 14 days, but they are then fed for a further three weeks, usually by the male. Robins often have a second brood later in the summer.

While many native birds are in decline, robin populations are stable, although many can die during a cold winter; putting out food such as mealworms, cheese, fat, crushed peanuts and dried fruit throughout these months can increase their chances of survival.

Identifying holly

Celebrated for its evergreen spiny leaves and bright red berries which prevail through the coldest season, holly is symbolic in the Christian church of Christ's thorny crown and the blood he shed on the cross, but its association with winter festivals dates back further to the time of the Druids, who also held the plant sacred. The common holly (*Ilex aquifolium*) and the Highclere holly (*Ilex × altaclerensis*), and their many cultivars, are the most widely available forms, while Japanese holly (*Ilex crenata*) has become increasingly popular for low hedging and cloud-pruning. Holly is dioecious, which means male and female flowers are produced on separate plants and, for berries, you will need a female with a male to pollinate it, although there are usually males growing in the wild nearby, so you may not need to buy one. This shrub thrives on most garden soils and in sun or part shade.

ILEX × ALTACLERENSIS 'LAWSONIANA' AGM
With its almost spineless green leaves, each decorated with a bold yellow splash, this female cultivar produces bunches of brown-red berries throughout the winter.
H x S: up to 8 x 8m (26 x 26ft)

ILEX AQUIFOLIUM 'ARGENTEA MARGINATA' AGM
The prickly cream-edged green leaves of this female cultivar combine with bright red berries to create a show-stopping picture in the winter garden.
H x S: up to 12 x 8m (39 x 26ft)

ILEX AQUIFOLIUM 'J.C. VAN TOL' AGM
A beautiful spineless female form, ideal for hedging, 'J.C. van Tol' produces green, glossy spiny leaves and bright red autumn and winter berries.
H x S: 6 x 4m (20 x 13ft)

ILEX AQUIFOLIUM 'HANDSWORTH NEW SILVER' AGM
This beautiful holly produces spiny cream-edged leaves and bright red berries from autumn and through winter. Plant with a male such as 'Blue Prince' for berries.
H x S: up to 8 x 3m (26 x 10ft)

ILEX × ALTACLERENSIS 'GOLDEN KING' AGM
Despite its name, 'Golden King' is a female holly with gold-edged, spineless green leaves and reddish-brown autumn berries that ripen to red.
H x S: up to 6 x 5m (20 x 16ft)

Garden tales

The glamorous poinsettia (*Euphorbia pulcherrima*) is one of the UK's most popular winter-season plants, sold at Christmas time when its scarlet leafy rosettes are used alongside tinsel and baubles to brighten up our homes. A native of Central America, this colourful perennial has been viewed as a holy flower in its homeland for many hundreds of years. Mexican folklore of the 16th century tells the tale of a poor young girl called Pipeta who brought a bouquet of weeds to present to the baby Jesus at Christmas, but when she placed her humble gift upon the altar they turned into poinsettias. They then became known as *Flores de Noche Buena* or "Flowers of the Holy Night" and were used to adorn nativity scenes.

The plant went unnoticed by the rest of the world until the early 19th century, when American botanist and physician Joel Roberts Poinsett brought it back from Mexico to the United States. It was then cultivated by Robert and Ann Bartram Carr at the famous Bartram's Botanic Garden in Philadelphia, and cuttings were later sent to James McNab, head gardener at the Edinburgh Botanic Garden, where it flowered for the first time in 1835. However, it was not until the late 20th century when nurseryman Paul Ecke Jr. sent free poinsettias to TV studios in the United States that the plant's popularity soared and it became widely used as a colourful festive flower.

Today, the poinsettia is regarded as the quintessential Christmas plant, mass cultivation in heated greenhouses making it widely available in the UK and within most people's price range. The elegant red rosettes are, in fact, leafy bracts, and the actual flowers are the small, yellow blooms in the centre of the foliage clusters; they are also available in cream, pink and white.

To keep your poinsettia happy, place it in a warm room, away from draughts, with indirect sunlight and temperatures above 13°C (55°F) day and night. Water regularly to keep the compost is damp, but not wet, and lightly mist the foliage every other day.

Legend: Yule

The winter solstice on the 21st–22nd December marks the shortest day of the year and has been celebrated for thousands of years by many cultures as the moment when the sun is reborn. It was traditionally known as Yule, the Anglo-Saxon word for sun and light, and is believed to have developed from the Ancient Norse festival of Jul. Celebrations lasted for 12 days, and included feasts, the lighting of bonfires and making sacrifices to the gods or other supernatural beings such as elves. Some historians think it was also when the Norse people gave offerings to Odin, the god of the dead, who was also known as Jolnir, while others say the festival was simply a celebration of the new year.

The first recording of Yule in Britain was in the 8th century by English monk and historian Bede, who described it as the beginning of 'giuli', a two-month period after the winter solstice when sunlight began to increase again. The festival and other pagan winter traditions were adopted by the church when Christianity came to Britain. Religious leaders made the 25th December a celebration of the birth of Christ, though the scriptures do not record the day itself, and the 12 days of Yule became the 12 days of Christmas, which represents the time between the birth of Christ and the coming of the Magi.

> Celebrations lasted for 12 days, and included feasts, the lighting of bonfires and making sacrifices to the gods or other supernatural beings such as elves.

Another ancient pagan tradition followed by early Christians was the burning of the Yule log on Christmas day. The log was usually an oak or ash branch that was kept from year to year and partly burned at sunset to protect the home from fire or lightning damage. The ashes were sprinkled on the fields after the festival to ensure a good harvest in the coming year, while the remaining log was stored for 12 months and used to rekindle the fire on the following Christmas day. Today, this tradition has been more commercialized and most of us now think of a Yule log as a chocolate Christmas cake.

Index

Picture credits

Abi Charge-Thornton © RHS 89; Ali Cundy © RHS 115 (7), 175 (4); Andrew Halstead © RHS 125; © Angela Harding 10, 30, 50, 70, 90, 110, 130, 150, 170, 190, 210, 230; anitapol / Shutterstock 26; Anna Brockman © RHS 115 (2); Anne Coatesy / Shutterstock 86; Barry Phillips © RHS 87t, 155 (10), 195 (11), 207tl; Calderson / Shutterstock 207br; Carol Sheppard © RHS 13b, 33t, 35 (1), 35 (3), 55 (6), 55 (9), 74, 75 (5), 75 (6), 92, 95 (3), 95 (4), 95 (6), 107mb, 147t, 147ml, 147mr, 155 (1), 163t, 173t, 175 (1), 175 (5), 183tr, 186, 195 (6), 195 (10), 227ml, 227b, 235 (8), 246; Caroline Beck © RHS 167tr; Cecile Moisan © RHS 115 (9), 187br; Christina Siow / Shutterstock 156; © Christopher Whitehouse 47tl; Claire Campbell © RHS 127ml, 147b; Clare Austin © Hardy Plants 55 (11); Clive Nichols © RHS 203b; Elvira Gr / Shutterstock 236; Fiona Lea © RHS 55 (7), 115 (5), 115 (6), 115 (10), 135 (4), 135 (10), 155 (6); GAP Photos / Mel Watson 76; Georgi Mabee © RHS 52t, 65, 165, 173b, 203tl, 241; Giedriius / Shutterstock 126; Giles Penfound © RHS 95 (10); © Gordon Rae 47tr, 47bl, 47br; Graham Titchmarsh © RHS 15 (8), 161, 247br; Guy Harrop © RHS 82m, 123bl, 235 (7); © Hardy's Cottage Garden Plants 115 (4); Helen Jermyn © RHS 63bl, 187tr; Helen Yates © RHS 63br, 183tl, 223b; Inga Gedrovicha / Shutterstock 29; Jacqui Hurst © RHS 101; Janet Cubey © RHS 187bl; Jason Ingram © RHS 15 (1), 43t, 52b, 63tr, 67mb, 67bm, 75 (10), 82b, 95 (8), 113tl, 132, 154l, 155 (5), 162, 194b, 214, 220b, 222; Joanna Kossak © RHS 15 (2), 35 (2), 35 (8), 67mt, 75 (1), 75 (7), 75 (8), 81, 87m, 95 (2), 115 (1), 127bl, 135 (7), 155 (2), 155 (7), 175 (7), 175 (9), 175 (10), 175 (11), 215 (2), 235 (5), 247tr, 247bl; Joe Wainwright © RHS 153t; John Trenholm © RHS 134, 172; Jon Enoch © RHS 174t; Jon Webster © RHS 195 (9); Juan Aceituno / Shutterstock 46; Julie Howden © RHS 221; Karol Waszkiewicz / Shutterstock 106; Korostylev Dmitrii / Shutterstock 73br; Lee Beel © RHS 35 (6); Leigh Hunt © RHS 15 (9), 15 (11), 95 (5), 95 (7), 107mt, 107bl; Lindsay Durrant © RHS / David Sisley – Straight Mile Nursery Gardens 75 (3); Liz Beal © RHS 245; Liz Grant © RHS 116; Lorna Trimnell © RHS 167br; Maddie Meddings © RHS 183br; Marie Teresa Clements 215 (11); Mark Bolton © RHS 55 (4), 163b, 175 (2), 196, 235 (10); Mark Winwood © Dorling Kindersley Ltd 28, 35 (9), 147mt, 155 (9), 207mr, 235 (2); Mark Winwood © RHS 15 (10), 68, 235 (11); © Michael John Day 243tl; Mike Sleigh © RHS 55 (10), 96, 143t, 195 (8), 215 (5), 215 (8); Nadiinko / Shutterstock recipe icons throughout Neil Hepworth © RHS 21, 23t, 23b, 25, 32, 34, 60, 63tl, 73tl, 93t, 100, 113tr, 114, 123tr, 141, 153br, 155 (8), 166, 176, 195 (2), 201l, 207bl, 220t, 223tl; Nicola Stocken © RHS 15 (3), 15 (7), 27tr, 27 ml, 27br, 55 (1), 55 (2), 75 (2), 75 (11), 115 (8), 135 (1), 135 (6), 135 (11), 155 (3), 155 (11), 175 (8), 195 (1), 215 (6), 215 (7), 235 (1), 235 (6), 235 (9), 247m; Olga Ponomarenko / Shutterstock 213tl; Paul Debois © RHS 55 (8), 75 (9), 115 (11), 136, 142, 195 (3); © Paul Harris 47m; © Peter Beales Roses 15 (5), 215 (10); Peter Turner Photography / Shutterstock 56; Philippa Gibson © RHS 95 (9), 95 (11), 195 (7), 215 (4), 247bm; qnula / Shutterstock 36; Rebecca Ross © RHS 83; © RHS 35 (11), 87bl, 87br, 105, 167mb, 167bl, 175 (3), 225, 227mr, 235 (4); RHS Lindley Collections 48, 88, 148, 149, 168; RHS Lindley Collections/Caroline Maria Applebee 49, 128; RHS Lindley Collections/Iris Humphreys 228; RHS Lindley Collections/Johann Simon Kerner 208; RHS Lindley Collections/John Frederick Miller 206; RHS Lindley Collections/Lydia Penrose 229; RHS Lindley Collections/Pieter van Kouwenhoorn 169; RHS Lindley Collections/Priscilla Susan Bury 248; RHS Lindley Collections/S. Watts/Augusta Withers 188; RHS Lindley Collections/Walter Hood Fitch 108; Richard Bloom © RHS 6–7, 35 (4), 180, 235 (3), 250–251; Rodney Lay © RHS 67t, 67br; Rudmer Zwerver / Shutterstock 226; Sara Draycott © RHS 27mb, 35 (5); Sarah Cuttle © RHS 123tl, 133tl, 133tr, 133bl, 135 (5); Sarycheva Olesia / Shutterstock 234t; Sheila Dearing © RHS 135 (8); Simon Bratt / Shutterstock 66; Simon Garbutt © RHS 195 (5), 203tr; Stefan Sutka / Shutterstock 146; Sue Drew © RHS 67bl, 167mt; tamu1500 / Shutterstock 107br; tan47 / Shutterstock 9; © Thorncroft Clematis 55 (5); Tim Sandall © RHS 12t, 12b, 13t, 15 (4), 15 (6), 22, 27mt, 33m, 33b, 35 (7), 40, 41, 43b, 45, 53t, 53m, 53b, 54, 55 (3), 73tr, 73bl, 75 (4), 82t, 87bm, 93b, 94, 103, 107tr, 113ml, 113bl, 113br, 115 (3), 121, 123br, 127tr, 127mr, 127br, 133br, 135 (2), 135 (3), 140, 143m, 143b, 153bl, 154r, 173m, 174b, 183bl, 187tl, 187mr, 193tl, 193tr, 193b, 194t, 195 (4), 201r, 213tr, 213b, 215 (1), 215 (3), 215 (9), 223tr, 227tr, 227m, 232, 233tl, 233tr, 233b; Wendy Wesley © RHS 135 (9), 175 (6), 207tr, 234b, 243tr, 243b; Wilf Halliday © RHS 35 (10); Zebrina Rendall © RHS 95 (1), 155 (4)